I0152498

All scriptures are from New King James Version of the Bible unless otherwise stated.

Published by
GOSPEL PENTECOSTAL ASSEMBLY
(The Glorious Family)
N0 5/7 Olusola Street, Off Union Road, Cement Bus Stop, Abeokuta Expressway, Dopemu, Lagos, Nigeria
P. O. Box 2328, Agege, Lagos
Tel. 08072888191
E-mail: johnsonadeyemi_rev@yahoo.com
Website: www.gpainternational.org
Face book: www.facebook.com/jbadeyemi
Blogsite: www.jbadeyemi.com
Twitter:@jbadeyemi

ISBN: 978-978-944-751 0

DEDICATION

This book is dedicated to

The glory of God
the Father, the Son, and the Holy Spirit,
the Author of new beginnings.

APPRECIATION

To God be the glory, the Author of new beginnings and Giver of wisdom who has bestowed on me great grace and deeper understanding of His ways and counts me worthy to be His workmanship in Christ Jesus created for good works.

I wish to express my profound thanks to the ministers, workers and entire members of this Commission, Gospel Pentecostal Assembly (the glorious family) for their steadfast love and support.

I am highly indebted to my editor, proof-readers and my secretary for their immense contributions without which the high quality of this book would not have been possible.

I thank my wife and children for their usual unflinching support and cooperation.

I thank the readers of my other books for their feedback, loyalty and suggestions which have become source of inspiration to me.

To all of you including the readers of this book, may you experience new beginnings in life, business and ministry in the name of Jesus. Amen.

CONTENTS

INTRODUCTION

A new thing is an event, an experience, a miracle or something that is unprecedented- a unique, uncommon, unusual thing; something that never happened before, an event that is totally distinct from the past in terms of power, glory, beauty and character. God's "new thing" supersedes all old and former things. It is something original, fresh and brand new.

In Isaiah 43: 19 - the main text for this book - God promised, through Prophet Isaiah, that: "I will do a new thing". This "new thing" will be fresh, brand new, unique and unprecedented. God, no doubt, had done "great things" in the past among His people (Psalm 126: 2-3). He can do "greater things than these" (John 1: 50), and use His servants to do "greater works" (John 14: 12), in this end time.

The Hebrew word used by Isaiah for "new" is chadash; it denotes that which is new, fresh. It is translated "fresh" only in Job 29: 20, where Job said, "My glory was fresh in me, and my bow was renewed in my hand". The New Testament equivalent Greek word is kainos which denotes new, in freshness. It is used "of that which is unaccustomed or unused, not new in time, recent, but new as to form or quality of different nature from what is contrasted as old". 1

Both the Old and New Testament words describe "new thing" as something unprecedented, an experience in contrast to "old things". This is expressed by Isaiah; "Remember ye not the former things, neither consider the things of old. Behold, I will do a new thing…" (Isa. 43: 18, 19).

The unprecedented nature of God's "new things" was demonstrated in the ministry of Joshua in the battle of five kings against Gibeon. Joshua's prayer suspended the solar system; he prayed for the sun to stand over Gibeon and the moon to stand in its place over the valley of Aijalon, and it was so (Josh 10: 12). We are told:

So the sun stood still, and the moon stopped, till the people had revenged upon their enemies. Is this not written in the Book of Jasher? So the sun stood still in the midst of heaven, and did not hasten to go down for about a whole day. (Joshua 10: 13)

1. W. E. Vine, *Vine's Expository Dictionary of New Testament Words*, Massachusetts: Hendrickson Publishers, (no date), p.791

In verse 14, it is recorded that there had never been a day like that before, when the Lord stopped the sun and the moon in answer to faith prayer.

And there has been no day like that, before it or after it, that the Lord heeded the voice of a man, for the Lord fought for Israel. (Joshua 10:14)

Although it was "a new thing" in Joshua's time, it was not new in Elijah's and Elisha's times- whose prayers overruled scientific laws. Elijah's prayer shut and opened heaven; it ceased to rain when he prayed and the rain fell when he prayed again (Jam. 5: 16- 18). Elisha's faith set aside the law of floatation when the lost axe head floated (2 Kings 6: 1- 7). Today, we have been given authority to cast out demons and "mountains" can be removed in response to faith.

God is a God of new things; He is always creating new things. Nothing is new, where God is concerned. What was "a new thing" yesterday may not be new today; for God is ahead of time and He is always doing new things- everyday.

Prophet Jeremiah spoke of the mercies- and, indeed, the works- of God that "are new every morning" (Lam. 3: 23 KJV) or "fresh each day" (LB) or "fresh each morning" (NLT). This implies that one can experience something new today, and wake up the next morning to discover that another brand "new thing" has happened. I seem to agree with the saying that: "wonders shall never end". This was what Jeremiah meant to convey in his lamentation.

They are new every morning; great is your faithfulness (Lamentation 3: 23)

Isaiah used the same Hebrew word for "new things", which describes its distinctiveness. In Isaiah 48:6, he wrote: "... I have made you hear new things..." God dignified and favoured His people with remarkable providence by showing them new things from one generation to another. He revealed to them new things through His prophets. He showed them new things by the prophets of their own day.

The distinctiveness of this "new things" is clearly revealed in the creation of a new world – a new earth and new heaven – which will be totally different from the past and present in nature, principle and order.

Writing on the glorious new creation, Isaiah said:

For behold, I create new heavens and a new earth; and the former shall not be remembered, or come to mind. Isaiah65:17

For as the new heaven and the new earth which I will make shall remain before Me says the Lord, so shall your descendants and your name remain. Isaiah66:22

The primary purpose of writing this book is to admonish Christians- and, indeed, the Church- concerning God's promise of "new things", prophesied by Isaiah. The promise is not exclusively for Israel, it also applies to the church. Secondly, the purpose is to challenge and motivate the church to believe God for new things, prepare for new things, expect new things and receive new things.

It is my earnest prayer that the contents of this book will become a reality in your life. As you read it, may you experience brand new things, new favours, new victories, new blessings, new open doors, new possibilities- in every area of your life, ministry and relationship. Moreover, I pray that you will receive a vision for new things, a new heart to pursue these new things, new strength to overcome new challenges, a fresh unction to function in the realm of new things and a new empowerment to do new and greater exploits.

Chapter 1

A BRAND NEW THING

About 712BC, God spoke through Prophet Isaiah, to His people that He would "do a new thing" (KJV), a "brand new thing" (LB) or "something new" (NLT). This promise marked a new beginning, a fresh start, a new chapter in the history of Israel. It is a promise of restoration, reconciliation in God's relationship with His ancient people.

This "new thing" would be fresh, different or distinct from all their previous blessings as God's people. Israel had seen great miracles, great deliverances, great victories, Divine leading and provisions in the wilderness (See Deut 9:16-18; Psalm 106:9-14; 107:33-36). But they would yet again experience a "new Exodus" which will take place through a "new wilderness".

All their past miracles would be nothing compared to the uncommon miracles which this "new thing" brings.

The Word of God declares:

Behold, I will do a new thing; now it shall spring forth; shall ye not know it? I will even make a way in the wilderness, and rivers in the desert. Isaiah 43:19 (KJV)

In the previous chapter, the Prophet had made a similar prediction:

Behold the former things are come to pass, and new things do I declare: before they spring forth I tell you of them. Isaiah 42:9 (KJV)

The Book of Isaiah is divided into two parts: The first part (Chapters 1-39) consists of warning of judgment over Israel and Judah and their neighbouring nations – Assyria, Babylon, Moab, Syria, Philistia, Edom, etc. God's people had become apostate and were to be judged for their sin- especially for trusting in foreign alliances. It speaks of the events leading to the captivity and reflects a relationship that has been marred – resulting in God's displeasure over His people. The second part (Chapters 40-66) consists of words of comfort, hope and assurance relating to events beyond the captivity and the future of God's people. It reflects a new beginning, a restored relationship with God.

God sends this comfort to His people, to reassure them of this restoration:

Comfort ye, comfort ye my people, saith your God. Speak ye comfortably to Jerusalem, and cry unto her, that her warfare is accomplished, that her iniquity is pardoned, for she hath received of the

LORD's hand double for all her sins Isaiah
40:1-2 (KJV)

A Fresh Start

In Isaiah 42, the prophet concludes with God's
sorrow over the moral and spiritual decay of
His people. It serves as a memento of their
"former" way of life, "former things" in their
relationship with God and God's displeasure for
their misdemeanour.

***Therefore, He has poured on him the fury
of His anger and the strength of battle; it
has set him on fire all around, yet he did
not take it to heart*** Isaiah 42:25

In chapter 43, however- notwithstanding their
failings and failures – God promises that He
would show them mercy, bring them back from
captivity and restore them. It opens a new
chapter and gives them a new opportunity for
a fresh start.

***But now, thus says the Lord, who created
you, O Jacob, and He who formed you, O
Israel: fear not, I have redeemed you; I
have called you by your name; you are
Mine. When you pass through the waters,
I will be with you; And through the rivers,
they shall not overflow you. When you
walk through the fire, you shall not be
burned.*** Isaiah 43:1-2

The opening conjunction "But now"- in spite of God's past judgment for Israel's sins – signifies that a new thing is about to happen; God will "do a new thing" (Isa. 43:19). Before or in the past, it was judgment, "but now" it is mercy, favour and restoration. This is a usual opening phrase to indicate a change in circumstances, a change from an old to a new; from Divine justice to Divine mercy; from Divine displeasure to Divine pleasure; it signifies willingness on God's part to forgive, forget and restore His people. This phrase, in spite of God's past just judgment, is common in Isaiah: "Come now and let us reason together" (Isa. 1:18); "Therefore thus saith the LORD God of hosts, O my people... be not afraid... For yet a very little while, and the indignation shall cease" (Isaiah 10:24-27); "yet now" (Isa. 44:1 KJV) or "But now" (NLT); "And now, saith the LORD... thou shalt no more drink it again: but I will..." (Isa. 51:21-23); "Now therefore ..." (Isa. 52:5).

The phrase is also used by other prophets to convey the same message: "Therefore, also now, saith the LORD, turn ye over to me with all your heart, and with fasting and with weeping, and with mourning... Then will I the LORD be jealous for His land and pity His people. Yea, the LORD will answer..." (Joel 2:12, 18, 19; See : Joel 2:12-32); "Yet now be strong... saith the LORD, and work; for I am with you, saith the LORD of hosts" (Hag. 2:4).

Why New Things?

God certainly has His purposes for doing or creating new things – not only in relation to His creatures, but also in relation to Himself. He does new things to demonstrate His mercy and forgiveness to His people, to give men opportunity for a new beginning, to demonstrate His sovereignty and faithfulness in keeping promises.

God will do new things primarily and ultimately for His own glory and honour. His glory is revealed through His creative acts.

Everyone who is called by My name, whom I have created for My glory, I have formed him, yes I have made him
Isa. 43:7

David declares:

The heaven declares the glory of God; and the firmament shows His handwork.
Psalm 19:1

Again, David said:

One generation shall praise Your works to another, and shall declare your mighty acts. I will meditate on the glorious splendour of Your majesty, and on Your wondrous works. Men shall speak of the might of Your awesome acts, and I will declare Your greatness. Psalm 145: 4-6

God is the creator and sustainer of everything. All the creatures in heaven and earth will sing praise to God, in recognition of this fact (Rev. 5:13). The chorus of the twenty four elders in heaven echoes the primary purpose of God in creation.

Thou art worthy, O Lord, to receive glory and honour and power: for thou has created all things, and for thy pleasure they are and were created Revelation 4:11 KJV

God has created all things – both the old things and the new things- for His pleasure. That is, God derives pleasure in creating new things for the benefit of His creatures, especially His children.

Do good in thy good pleasure unto Zion: build thou the walls of Jerusalem Psalm 51:18 KJV

For the LORD taketh pleasure in his people: he will beautify the meek with salvation Psalm 149:4 KJV

Declaring the end from the beginning, and from ancient times the things that are not yet done, saying, my counsel shall stand,

and I will do all my pleasure Isaiah 46:10 KJV

In the book of Isaiah, God's purpose for doing new things is revealed twice; first in chapter 41:20 and in chapter 43:20.

In Isaiah 41:18-19, we are told:

I will open rivers in desolate heights, and fountains in the midst of the valleys; I will make the wilderness a pool of water, and the dry land springs of water. I will plant in the wilderness the cedar and the acacia tree; the myrtle and the oil tree. I will set in the desert the cypress tree and the pine and the box tree together Isaiah 41:18-19

Then, in verse 20, it says:

That they may see and know, and consider, and understand together, that the hand of the LORD has done this, and the Holy One of Israel has created it Isaiah 41:20 KJV

According to Isaiah 43:20, God's purpose is that all creatures will honour and glorify Him. Every creature – including the wild beasts – will praise God for giving them water in the desert and making rivers in the dry wasteland.

The Psalmist confirms this when he said, "Let everything that hath breath praise the LORD"

(Psalm 150:6). Everything that has breath implies all creatures – including the wild animals of the field – will express gratitude and honour to the Living God.

Praise the Lord from the earth, you great sea creatures and all the depths; fire and nail, snow and clouds; stormy wind, fulfilling His word. Mountains and all hills, fruitful trees and all cedars; beasts and all cattle; creeping things and flying fowl. Kings of the earth and all peoples; princes and all judges of the earth; both young men and maidens; old men and children. Let them praise the name of the Lord, for His name alone is exalted Psalm 148:7-13

All the creatures of God – "all his works in all places of his dominion" (Psa. 103:22), in heaven and on earth and under the earth, will bless, glorify and honour God.

And every creature which is in heaven and on the earth and under the earth and such as in the sea, and all that are in them, I heard saying: "Blessing and honour and glory and power be to Him who sits on the throne, and to the Lamb, forever and ever!" Revelation 5:13

Truly, God is the author of new things. He is the originator and source of all things; He owns everything because He created everything both in heaven and on earth. God is full of supernatural surprises and He is ready to do new things in your life, if only you believe, obey, accept and trust Jesus Christ as your Lord and Saviour.

From today, you will begin to experience new things in your life, family, business and finances. Surely, Jesus will do a new thing as He has promised, ask and trust Him for new things and you will have them (Mark 11: 24).

This is a new day and a new dawn in your life.

Chapter 2

THE ESSENTIAL ELEMENTS OF THIS NEW THING

According to Isaiah 43:19, the promise of God to do "a new thing" comprises four distinctive elements, which make the promise certain and reassuring.

1.   The promise: "I will do a new thing"

2.   It shall spring forth

3.   I will make a way in the wilderness

4.   Rivers in the desert.

a.   I Will Do A New Thing

"I will do a new thing" is God's promise of assurance, hope and comfort for you; it is a promise that God will do something new in your life that will positively impact your relationship, ministry and community. It is a brand new thing, something unprecedented in its nature or character. This miracle will bring a change in the totality of your being and in your destiny. It will lift you up to a new and higher realm and divinely put you on a new platform of unique and unlimited opportunities in your life and ministry. This was perhaps what David had in mind when he said:

I waited patiently for the Lord, and He heard my cry. He also brought me up out of horrible pit, out of the miry clay, and set my feet upon a rock, and established my steps. He has put a new song in my mouth- praise to our God; many will see it and fear, and will trust in the Lord. Psalm 40:1-3

Expect a new thing today – in your life, marriage, ministry and business; expect a new touch from God, a new opening and a new song. He will do as He has promised; your expectation for a new thing will not be disappointed.

For surely there is a hereafter, and your hope will not be cut off

Proverbs 23:18

b.   It Shall Spring Forth

A new thing has already begun; it is happening now; "now it shall spring forth" or "See, I have already begun" (NLT). It will spring forth as a germinating herb, sprouting with fresh and beautiful leaves and increasing, growing strong. This is a beautiful picture of a silent, but sure gradual growth of God's work in the life of a Christian. It may not be visible in the physical realm, yet it has begun to grow, gradually growing, like a seed in the ground; with time, it will manifest in the physical realm, bringing joy to the Believer. This is perfectly illustrated in the parable of the secretly growing seed:

And he said, "the kingdom of God is as if a man should scatter seed on the ground, and should sleep by night and rise by day, and the seed should sprout and grow, he himself does not know how. For the earth yields crops by itself: first the blade, then the head, after that the full grain in the head..." Mark 4: 26-28

The Hebrew word used for "spring forth" is instructive and interesting in its various usages. It is from the word tsamach, which denotes to bear, to spring forth, to sprout, to bud, to grow.

The word "spring forth" also means to "leap" – to grow by leaps and bounds. It also means to appear suddenly, unexpectedly and surprisingly. That is, to "cause to act suddenly by means of a spring, produce or develop suddenly or unexpectedly ..."2 This definition reveals some profound truths about new things springing forth: God is able to do beyond all our expectations (Eph. 3:20); God's miracles sometimes come unexpectedly – with pleasant surprises (Psalm 126:1-6); God's long awaited miracles usually come suddenly – unexpectedly and surprisingly – though silently developing underground, waiting for the perfect timing (Hab. 2:3).

The word is used for "spring forth" in Isaiah 42:9, for the springing forth of new things, in the same sense as it is used in Isaiah 43:19.

Behold, the former things are come to pass, and new things do I declare; before they spring forth I tell you of them Isaiah 42:9 KJV

It is also used of the speedy restoration of health, in answer to prayer and fasting.

Then shall thy light break forth as the morning, and thine health shall spring forth speedily: and thy righteousness shall go before thee; the glory of the LORD shall be thy re-reward Isaiah 58:8 KJV

It is used for growth: To grow means to increase, develop, expand and enlarge or become bigger. It is used for the growth of plants, trees, herbs and grass.

He causeth the grass to grow for the cattle, and herb for the service of man: that he may bring forth food out of the earth (Psalm 104:14 KJV; See also Gen. 2:9; Exod. 10:5; Psa. 147:8).

....

2 The Concise Oxford English Dictionary, Oxford University Press, London: 1961, P. 1242

It is used to describe the restoration of Samson's hair after it had been shaved. We are told that his hair began to grow again:

Howbeit the hair of his head began to grow again after he was shaven Judges 16:22 KJV

This presents a beautiful picture of "a new thing", a fresh start, for a humiliated giant. It also presents a clean picture of restoration, renewal, repair and rebuilding which characterize the "new things" promised by God. Samson's character was marred, but God made him again (see Jer. 18:1-4); though he was humiliated and defeated, but God honoured and developed him again; though he was shaved, his hair began to grow again – new things began to happen in his life; as his hair began to grow again, Samson prayed again, fought again and won again. His new experience gave him fresh zeal, and fresh strength to do greater exploits at the moment of his death than he did during his entire life time. Truly, his "new thing" lifted Samson from a zero to a hero and from a failure to a fulfilled man.

Then Samson said, "let me die with the Philistines! And he pushed with all his might, and the temple fell on the lords and all the people who were in it. So the

dead that he killed at his death were more than he had killed in his life Judges 16:30

It is used for bud: God promised to make the horn of David to bud (Psalm 132:17), that is, He will increase the power of David (NLT) or David's power shall grow (LB). God has also promised to water the ground and cause it to bring forth and bud, so that it can produce seed for the sower and food for the hungry (Isa. 65:10).

God is the source of our strength and the giver of "power to make wealth" (Deut 8:18). He will anoint you with fresh oil and make your "horn" bud and become stronger than your enemies. Thus you will increasingly grow in power and strength for uncommon exploits and supernatural breakthroughs in battle and ministry. Perhaps this was what David had in mind when he said:

But my horn shall thou exalt like the horn of a unicorn: and I shall be anointed with fresh oil Psalm 92:10

As you begin to experience "new things" from God, your "horn" will "bud" and you will be exalted above your enemies. Thus, you will rejoice in God's victory and sing a new song. In Hannah's Thanksgiving Song to God, she said:

My heart rejoice in the Lord; My horn is exalted in the Lord. I smile at my enemies, because I rejoice in Your salvation 1 Samuel 2:1

c. A New Pathway Through The Wilderness

Another new thing that God has promised to do is that He "will make a way in the wilderness" (KJV) or "make a pathway through the wilderness" (NLT) or "make a road through the wilderness" (LB). God had made a way in the past for Israel; He divided the Red Sea for them to pass through; He made a way in the wilderness between the Red Sea and their Promised Land; He even divided the Jordan River so that they passed through dry ground. But this "new" miracle of deliverance will be unique, unparalleled, and will be attended with the manifestation of God's power and favour.

God is a way Maker; He makes a way where there is no way. He can make a way in difficult places; He can level our seemingly high mountains (Isa. 40:4; Zech. 4:7); break down your "Jericho walls" (Jos 6:20); dry up your uncrossable seas and rivers and demolish your strong and mighty iron gates (Isaiah 45:2) and lead you through every strong iron door that has hitherto remained closed against your progress (Psa. 24:7-10; See also: Acts 12:10).

Making "a way in the wilderness" also implies opening new doors. God opens doors that no one can shut, and shuts doors that no one can open (Rev. 3:7-10). He shuts old doors, so that He may open new doors- better, bigger and more productive doors.

I will make each of My mountains a road, and My highways shall be elevated Isaiah 49:11

A new door is about to open – this door will surpass all your past old doors, in glory, beauty and greatness. It will lead to unlimited possibilities and usher you into a new realm in heavenly places. This door will open miraculously of its own accord and lead you to your new realm of supernatural breakthroughs.

When they were past the first and the second guard posts, they came to the iron gate that leads to the city, which opened to them of its own accord; and they went out and went down one street, and immediately the angel departed from him Acts 12:10

d.   Rivers In the Desert

A desert is a dry waste land - an uninhabited, uncultivated, hopelessly dry, and barren land. But God can create an "oasis", turning your barren land into a fertile, fruitful and productive land. He has promised to create "rivers in the desert" or "rivers in the dry wasteland" (NLT).

God can water your dry ground and turn your desert into a fertile, watered land (Psa. 107:35). Thus, you become increasingly fruitful and thrive like watered grass, like willows on a river bank.

Prophet Isaiah declares:

I will open rivers in desolate heights, and fountains in the midst of the valleys; I will make the wilderness a pool of water, and the dry land springs of water Isaiah 41:18

Again, he said:

For I will also pour water on him who is thirsty, and floods on the dry ground; I will pour My Spirit on your descendants, and My blessing on your offspring. Isaiah 44:3

God can bless you again, as He begins to do "new things" in your life; He can transform your barren wilderness into a beautiful garden, so that you can rejoice again and sing a new song.

The Lord will comfort Zion, He will comfort all her waste places; He will make her wilderness like Eden, and her desert like the garden of the Lord Isaiah 51:3

God can do again, what He did for you before, even better and bigger than all you experienced before (Ezek 36:11). This is what makes it "new" – a new thing indeed. As part of this new thing, God will divinely plant you like a tree along a river bank, so that you can grow increasingly and produce fruits seasonally.

He shall be like a tree planted by the rivers of water, that brings forth its fruit in its season, whose leaf also shall not wither; and whatever he does shall prosper Psalm 1:3

The Psalmist writes again

The righteous shall flourish like a palm tree, He shall grow like a cedar in Lebanon. Those who are planted in the homes of the Lord shall flourish in the courts of our God. They shall bear fruit in old age; they shall be fresh and flourishing. Psalm 92:12-14

Water is a symbol of life, wealth, health, Holy Spirit and reproduction. Water makes dry lands to thrive, brings prosperity in poverty and heals barrenness.

For I will give you abundant water for your thirst parched fields. And I will pour out My Spirit and my blessings on your

children. They shall thrive like watered grass, like willows on a river bank Isa. 44:3 Living Bible

I pray that you will be part of the new things God is doing in this end time; that every area of barrenness in your life – spiritually, biologically, ministerially, emotionally, morally and financially – will be healed. I command the curse of barrenness, over your marriage and ministry, to be reversed, in Jesus' Name (Exd. 23:26; Deut. 7:14 Gal. 3:13). From henceforth your ground shall no more be dry and barren (2 King 2:19-21).The God who makes barren women to raise children (Psa. 113:9), will make you productive; thus, you will rejoice and sing a new song (1 Sam. 2:5; Isa. 54:1)

Chapter 3

SEASON OF NEW THINGS

A season is a proper time, a suitable time, a time of favourable opportunity. It is the right time at which we normally receive an expected favour – such as: a bountiful harvest, rain, children, marriage, abundant blessings, period of usefulness, special breakthrough or something worth celebrating.

Naturally, we normally expect these things to happen at their appropriate seasons. As the Word of God declares:

And he shall be like a tree planted by the rivers of water, that brings forth its fruit in its season: whose leaf also shall not wither, and whatever he does shall prosper Psalm 1:3

We become disappointed when our expectations at a certain season are not fulfilled (see Matt 21:18-20 see also Mark 11:12-14). This was the case of Israel, when they were disappointed at the season of harvest.

The harvest is past, the summer is ended, and we are not saved. Jeremiah 8:20

My prayer for you is that your expectation for this season will not be disappointed (See Prov. 23:13); you will not miss your season, and you will bring forth your fruits at the appropriate seasons. I also pray that God will restore all your lost seasons (Joel 2:25) and give you double for all your wasted seasons (Job 42: 10, 12; Isa. 61:7; Zech. 9:12).

A Right Season For Everything

There is a season for every event in this life. This truth is profoundly stated by Solomon: "To everything there is a season and a time to every purpose under heaven" (Eccl. 3:1). Again, he said, "there is a time for every purpose and for every work" (Eccl. 3:17).

The Hebrew words used for "season" have various connotations and are more often used for "time". The Hebrew word used for "season" in Eccl. 3:1 is Zeman, which denotes an appointed occasion. It is used for "season" (Eccl. 3:1) and for set time or appointed time (Neh. 2:6; Esth. 9:27, 31). Of all the words used for "season" in the Old Testament, eth and mowadah are the most commonly used terms. The former, eth denotes time, due season. It is used for "season" fifteen times; "Then will I give you rain in due season" (Lev. 26:4; See also Deut 11:14; 28:12); "They are bearing fruit each season" (Psa. 1:3 NLT; see also: Psa. 104:27; 145:15 etc).

It is also used for time appointed (Gen.18:14; 2 Sam. 24:15), accepted time (Psalm 68:13), according to the time of life (2 King4:16, 17) or time. In Psalm 102:13, David declared, "Thou shalt arise, and have mercy on Zion: for the time to favour her, yea the set time has come." The time to favour Zion is the season of favour or a favourable season. David said, "It is time, for thee, LORD, to work" (Psa. 119: 126) and, according to Hosea, "It is time to seek the LORD" (Hosea 10:12). These scriptures clearly speak of appropriate times or favourable times – the right seasons and favourable seasons to seek God and to experience His power. This right timing is the season of favour. Prophet Isaiah confirmed this when he says, "Seek the LORD while you can find Him. Call on Him now while He is near" (Isa. 55:6 NLT).

The second word, mowadah, is used for seasons (Gen 1:14; Lev. 23:4; Psa. 104:19), due season (Num. 28:2), appointed season (Num. 9:2, 3, 7, 13). Elisha prophesied to the Shunamite: "About this season, according to the time of life, thou shalt embrace a son" (2 King 4:16). This prophecy was fulfilled: "And the woman conceived, and bare a son at that season that Elisha had said unto her, according to the time of life" (2 King 4:17).

I prophesy to you that about this season, according to the time of life, all your aspirations and expectations shall be fulfilled, you will experience all round fruitfulness, your reproach and shame shall be turned to testimony and the joy of the Lord shall be your strength.

In the New Testament, the most commonly used word is kairos. It denotes an occasion, a set time or due time, proper time, season or due season. It is used for season as follows: "fruits in their seasons" (Matt. 21:41) or "fruitful season" (Acts 14:17); "give them meat in due season" (Matt. 24:45) or for spiritual harvest: "for in due season we shall reap if we faint not" (Gal 6:9); a proper time for prophetic fulfillment: "my words, which shall be fulfilled in their season" (Luke 1:20); a time suitable for a purpose: "And when the devil had ended all the temptation he departed from him for a season" (Luke 4:13); times and seasons reserved by God: "It is not for you to know the times or seasons" (Acts 1:7), "But of the times and seasons... ye have no need that I write unto you" (1 Thes 5:1); the season of miracles: "For an angel went down at a certain season into the pool, and troubled the water" (John 5:4).

The same word kairos, is translated "time", with the same meaning as "season". It is used for time of harvest or harvest season: "and in the time of harvest I will say to the reapers..." (Matt. 13:30), "And when the time of the fruit drew near..." (Matt. 21:34); a season of reward for spiritual investments: "But he shall receive an hundredfold now in this time..." (Mark 10:30); the season of Divine visitation: "because thou knowest not the time of thy visitation" (Luke 19:44); a season of refreshing (Acts 3:19).

It is interesting also to note that kairos is translated "opportunity" (in Gal. 6:10 and Heb 11:15). There is an opportunity (or season) for doing the right thing with great results or rewards: "As we have therefore opportunity, let us do good unto all men, especially unto them who are of the household of faith" (Gal. 6:10 KJV).

Paul teaches us the importance of making good use of opportunities - to discover opportunities and make the best use of them. In verse 6, he says, "for in due season we shall reap, if we faint not" (Gal. 6:9). As discussed earlier, "season" and "opportunity" are derived from the same Greek word kairos. Thus, making the best and timely use of opportunities brings a timely harvest, in its appropriate season.

Success is achieved when we make the most of every opportunity we have to do what is necessary. This is the path of wisdom; a wise Christian discerns opportunities –even in the midst of difficulties- and makes the most of them. According to Albert Einstein: "In the middle of difficulty lies opportunity"[3]

Paul admonished:

See that ye walk circumspectly, not as fools, but as wise. Redeeming the time, because the days are evil   Eph. 5:15, 16 KJV

In other versions, "Redeeming the time" is translated, "Make the most of every opportunity" (NLT and LB).

Opportunity is a favourable time, favourable chance or a good chance, an opening for action. Divinely initiated opportunities make room for unlimited possibilities

Alexander Graham Bell says:

When one door closes another door opens; but we so often look so long and so regretfully upon the closed door, that we do not see the ones which are opened for us [4]

Opportunity is the key to your breakthrough, a door to your uncommon miracles. But it does not come "all the time," you may not have a better opportunity, if you fail to make the most of it. It was Jimmy Cliff, the Jamaican singer, who said, "Opportunity knocks only but once, grab it now or you lose your chance".

....

3. *The New Encyclopedia of Christian Quotations, Hampshire: John Hunt Publishing Ltd; 2000, P. 704*

There is much truth in what Cliff said; although you may have several opportunities, your attitude to a great opportunity can determine your destiny. John of the cross said:

If you lose an opportunity you are like one who lets the bird fly away: you never get it back. [5]

Napoleon Bonaparte was right when he said: "Ability is of little account without opportunity" 6. It is not your ability, but your availability at the right place, at the right timing. By trying to be at the right place, at the right season will open doors of unlimited opportunities. Those who are divinely positioned, in His timing, "are like trees planted along the river bank, bearing fruit each season" Psalm 1:3 NLT).

Solomon made a profound statement to confirm this truth:

I returned and saw under the sun - that, the race is not to the swift, nor the battle to the strong, nor bread to the wise, nor riches to men of understanding, nor favour to men of skill; but time and chance happen to them all Ecclesiastes 9:10

Take note of the link between "time" – season – and "chance" – opportunity.

....

4   *Ibid, P. 703*
5   *Ibid, P. 704*
6   *Ibid*

There are favourable opportunities at the right season. Make the most of your opportunity to maximize your effectiveness at your appropriate season. You are not where you are by "chance" or by accident; you have been divinely planted and divinely located at the right place and season, to achieve greatness and make great impacts in your generation "for such a time as this" (Esth. 4:14).

The righteous shall flourish like palm tree, he shall grow like a cedar in Lebanon. Those that be planted in the house of the Lord shall flourish in the courts of our God. They shall still bring forth fruit in old age; they shall be fat and flourishing Psalm 92:12-14 KJV

Dear reader, this is your time, chance, opportunity and season, don't allow it to slip from your hands, seize it because this is the opportunity you have been waiting for. Remember, time waits for no one, strike when the iron is hot and you will surely breakthrough in this season of new things. This is your time!

Chapter 4

A NEW BEGINNING

God is the God of new beginnings: In Him there are opportunities for new beginnings and new beginners. He is not only the God of the beginning (Gen. 1:1; Rev. 1:8; 21:6), but also a God who originates or initiates new beginnings. This new beginning is a fresh start, a brand new start which allows for a second chance, creates new opportunities, opens new doors and gives us new hopes and a fresh start in our relationship with God.

A new beginning with God is a totally new experience which is distinct from and better than former experiences. It is a fresh start which closes every unfavourable door of negativities and failures and opens new doors to new favours, positive experiences and unlimited possibilities. We are divinely ushered into a new realm of supernatural relationship with God where we experience new joy, new things and sing new songs.

Behold, the former things are come to pass, and new things do I declare ... Sing unto the LORD a new song, and his praise from the end of the earth ... Isa. 42:9-10

The Passover marked a new beginning of Israel's breakthrough. It marked the end of their exile and the beginning of their exodus to their promised land.

When it was time for God to deliver His people from their land of oppression and take them to their promised land, He initiated a change in their calendar and gave them a new beginning- a new beginning in the history of Israel and the fulfillment of redemptive promises.

This month shall be unto you the beginning of months: it shall be the first month of the new year to you Exod. 12:2 KJV.

In ancient times, in God's relationship with Israel, God often made promises of a fresh new beginning. Each new start was progressively better than the previous. Each new beginning is distinctively of "a better end"- a better end than the former beginning. According to Solomon: "Better is the end of a thing than the beginning thereof..." (Eccl.7:8 KJV). This is more profoundly and clearly expressed by Prophet Ezekiel; he wrote:

And I will multiply you man and beast; and they shall increase and bring fruit; and I will settle you after your old estates, and I will do better unto you than at your beginnings; and ye shall know that I am the LORD Ezek. 36:11 KJV.

It is encouraging and instructive to note that God has promised that: "I will do better unto you than your beginnings". It is also worth noting that the Prophet spoke of "your beginnings" –that is in plural- which is suggestive of previous numerous beginnings. But in comparison with all other "previous beginnings", God will initiate a fresh new beginning which will be better than all previous beginnings. God can initiate a brand-new beginning in your life- including your relationship, family, ministry and business- that will surpass all your past experiences. God can divinely give you an opportunity for a fresh start that will change your history and give you better hopes for your future and destiny.

The Hebrew word used for better is towb, which is used in a variety of ways in the Old Testament. It is used for good, better, more, most, good things, goodness, favour, wealth, pleasant, beautiful, prosperity. In other versions, it is rendered "more prosperous": "I will do you more prosperous than you were before" (NLT) or "I will do even more for you than I did before" (LB).

God's promise of a new beginning for you is for "better things", to make you "more than" you have ever had in your life. It is a new beginning that will divinely usher you into a fresh realm of supernatural breakthroughs, favours and exploits. It will take you into better places and give you better fruits, better results, better rewards, better ministry and transform your relationship from "bitter" to "better" and lift you from the worst to the best level.

"God is able to do exceeding abundantly above all" (Eph. 3:20) your expectations and lift you far beyond all your past levels and limitations. Better things come with a new beginning with God. A new beginning with God gave Jonah "a second chance" and fresh passion for service (Jonah 2:3, 4); it gave Isaiah a new vision of God (Isa. 6:1-8) and gave Samson a fresh anointing for exploits (Judges 16:22-30). In answer to prayer, God gave Jabez a fresh start, with a fresh touch, resulting in being lifted from the lowest to the highest, from the worst to the best, from the most dishonourable to the most honourable. We are told: "And Jabez was more honourable than his brethren" (1 Chro. 4:9). Formerly, he lived with a curse of sorrow, because his mother gave birth to him in sorrow. But his new beginning with God changed his past and ushered him into the path of a better destiny.

The "new beginning" is also described as "the latter end" which promises better things. This is best described in the words of Elihu, one of Job's friends:

Though your beginning was small, yet your latter end would increase abundantly
Job 8:7

Elihu's prediction was divinely fulfilled when God restored Job. Job's restoration gave him a new beginning, which was better than all his former blessings.

We are told:

And the Lord restored Job's losses when he prayed for his friends. Indeed the Lord gave Job twice as much as he had before. Job 42:10

In verse 12, it says:

Now the Lord blessed the latter days of Job more than his beginning; for he had fourteen thousand sheep, six thousand camels, one thousand female donkeys Job 42: 12

A new beginning with God opens a new chapter in your life, making your past "history". God has power to change your past and give you a brand-new beginning, a new opportunity to shine again, serve again and rejoice again – even better than it had been before. He can put an end to your weeping, turn the tears of your past into joy and your mourning into dancing.

For His anger is but for a moment, His favour is for life, weeping may endure for

a night, but joy comes in the morning
Psalm 30:5

You have turned for me my mourning into dancing. You have put off my sackcloth and clothed me with gladness   Psalm 30:11

I pray that the Lord will turn your pain to gain, your trial to triumph, your sorrow to joy, your weeping to celebration and your mourning to dancing, in Jesus name.

Chapter 5

FORGET FORMER THINGS

In Isaiah 43, the prophet declares:

Remember ye not the former things, neither consider the things of old Isa. 43:18 KJV

This text is directly and inseparably linked with our main verse, verse 19; they are both connected to present a complete picture, in the overall context of God's promise to do a new thing. The 18th verse is a step that leads to verse 19; it tells us what we must do in order to experience God's promise of verse 19.

First, we must "remember not" – that is, forget all – the former things. Secondly, do not consider or think over the things of old. Both "the former things" and "old things" must be forgotten, so that they can be replaced with new things – a new beginning that will surpass all old beginnings (Ezek 36:11).

Things To Remember

There are things we need to remember – and never forget; we need to remember past exploits, so that we can face our challenges with confidence (Josh. 14:1-12; I Sam. 17:34-37). We need to remember things that are necessary for our growth, wellbeing, usefulness, that will strengthen our faith in God and develop our relationship with Him. Moreover, we need to remember the past, so that we can avoid repeating past mistakes and make progress in life. Remembering some things of the past can keep us humble and more dependent on God. We remember them to help us know where we are coming from, why we are where we are and where we are heading to.

In the book of Deuteronomy, the children of Israel were constantly admonished to remember – and not forget – their roots, God's covenant with them and the mighty works wrought by God on their behalf.

He charges them to be very strict and careful in their observance of the law. "Only take heed to thyself, and keep thy soul diligently, lest thou forget the things which thine eyes have seen" (Deut. 4:9KJV). "Take you therefore good heed unto yourselves "(Verse 15). "Take heed unto yourselves, lest ye forget the covenant of the Lord your God which He made with you..." verse 23. In Deut. 7:18, God told Israel not to be afraid of their enemies: "Thou shalt not be afraid of them: but shalt well remember what the LORD thy God did unto Pharaoh, and unto all Egypt" (JKV). God told them to "remember all the way which the LORD thy God led thee all these forty years in the wilderness to humble thee..." (Deut. 8:2 KJV). "Beware that thou forget not the Lord thy God, in not keeping His commandments and His judgment, and His statutes, which I command thee this day" (Deut 8: 11 KJV). Moses concluded: "But thou shalt remember the LORD thy God: for it is he that giveth thee power to get wealth …" verse 18

In the Song of Moses, he said:

Remember the days of old, consider the years of many generations. Ask your father, and he will show you; your elders, and they will tell you when the Most High divided their inheritance to the nations, when He separated the sons of Adam, He set the boundaries of the peoples according to the number of the children of Israel. For the Lord's portion is His people; Jacob is the place of His inheritance Deuteronomy 32:7-9

David's remembrance of his past exploits gave him the confidence, faith and courage to fight Goliath.

Moreover David said: "The Lord who delivered me from the paw of the lion and from the paw of the bear, He will deliver me from the hand of this Philistine". And Saul said to David; "Go and the Lord be with you" I Samuel 17: 37

David was motivated to reach out to God, because he remembered the glorious miracles of the past (Psalm 143: 5-6). The same God who helped and blessed us in the past can do so again, even more than before. This is why we remember past miracles and answer to prayers, so that we can believe God for more breakthroughs.

Forget Old Things

On the other hand, however, there are things we must forget in order to experience new things and move to the next level. Remembering the past can hinder your progress; those who live on their past cannot actualize their destiny. We must let go the past, to reach out for new things. Isaiah admonished the children of Israel to: "Remember not the former things, neither consider the things of old".

The former things refer to Israel's past experience of Divine miracles, victories and deliverances. They refer to the events described in the preceding verses (Isa. 43:15-17) in the theocratic dispensations, when God was their King (verse 15), when He miraculously brought them out of the land of bondage and led them through the wilderness (verses 16-17). But they must forget all that – it is nothing compared with what God is going to do.

Why Forget Old Things?

There are many reasons – spiritual, moral, natural reasons - why we need to forget the past and move on with faith and expectation towards better things.

A. **God forgives and forgets our sins**

No more shall every man teach the neighbour, and every man his brother, saying: "Know the Lord, for all shall know Me, from the least of them to the greatest of them, says the Lord. For I will forgive their iniquity and their sin I will remember no more" Jeremiah 31:34

If God forgives and forgets our past failures, we, too, must learn to forgive – ourselves and others – and forget old things – old hurts, wounds, failures, disappointments, frustration, rejection, oppression and negativities.

b. **God has rolled away our old reproach**

Then the Lord said to Joshua, "this day I have rolled away the reproach of Egypt from you". Therefore the name of the place is called Gilgal to this day Joshua 5:9

The circumcision of the children of Israel symbolically rolled away the reproach of Egypt; they were thereby owned by God as the free-born children of God, having the seal of the covenant of their flesh and so the reproach of their bondage in Egypt was removed. They were tainted with the idolatry of Egypt, and that was their reproach, but now that they were circumcised it was to be hoped they would be so entirely devoted to God that the reproach of their affection to Egypt would be rolled away. Their coming safely to Canaan rolled away the reproach of Egypt, for it silenced that spiteful suggestion of the Egyptians that "for mischief they were brought out, the wilderness had shut them in" (Exod. 14:3). Their wandering for forty years in the wilderness confirmed the reproach, but now that they had entered Canaan in triumph that reproach was done away.

When God glorifies Himself in perfecting the salvation of His people, He not only silence the reproach of their enemies, but rolls it upon themselves. We are expected to live above sin so that it will not have dominion over us. We should not roll it back on ourselves again the shame and burden that the Lord had taken off our neck when our sins were forgiven.

c. Forget the past and move forward
The approach of Egyptian army terrified the children of Israel and they placed heavy pressure on Moses to handle the crisis. They

looked back and become terrified. Looking back can cause fear and defeat. Moses did not panic since he had seen the power of God's handwork in Egypt. Instead, he exuded both poise and peace, winning for himself great credibility as a leader. Moses projected clarity and confidence instead of confusion. "And the Lord said to Moses; "why do you cry to Me? Tell the children of Israel to go forward" (Exod. 14:15)

With single –minded passion, Paul defined the goal and determined how to get it, he forgot the past and pursued the prize of the call.

Not that I have already attained, or I am already perfected, but I press on, that I may lay hold of that for which Christ Jesus has also laid hold of me. Brethren, I do not count myself to have apprehended, but one thing I do, forgetting those things which are behind and reaching forward to those things which are ahead. I press toward the goal for the prize of the upward call of God in Christ Jesus. Philippians 3:12 -14

d.   We are now new creatures: Old things have passed away

Paul wrote:

Therefore, if anyone is in Christ, he is a new creation: old things have passed

away, behold all things have become new.
2 Corinthians 5:17

The old Adamic nature has been submerged by the new nature of Christ which does not sin (1 John 3:4-6). The old things being the desires of the flesh (Gal. 5:19-21) have been destroyed by the new nature when we take on the new nature of Christ.

Christians glory only in the cross of Christ, having become new creation, not in religion, status, race, circumcision, law or self-righteousness.

For in Christ Jesus neither circumcision nor uncircumcision avails nothing but a new creation Galatians 6:15

e.   We are under a new covenant

The new covenant is a better ministry established by a better Mediator and established on the better promises (Heb. 8:6). God now writes His law in the heart of the believer, not just on the stone tablet.

Paul wrote on the new covenant:

But when God found fault with the people, he said: "The day is coming, says the LORD, when I will make a new covenant with the people of Israel and Judah. This new covenant will not be like the one I made with their ancestors... But this is the new covenant I will make... I will put my laws in their minds, and I will write them on their hearts... Heb.8:9-10 NLT

The blood of Jesus, the seal of the new covenant, is a better blood which cries for forgiveness unlike the blood of Abel which cried for vengeance.

To Jesus the Mediator of the new covenant and to the blood of sprinkling that speaks better things than that of Abel Hebrews 12:24

f.   New wine must be put into new bottles

Nor do they put new wine into old wineskins, or else the new wineskins break, the wine is spilled, and the wineskins are ruined. But they put new wine into new wineskins, and both are preserved Matthew 9:17

Jesus' statement here is to the effect that the new covenant is under proper scrutiny to prevent it from being adulterated by the old covenant which involved ceremonial practices. If there was no defect in the old covenant there would not be a need for the new covenant.

g. We must renounce our former ways of life

That you put off, concerning your former conduct, the old man which grows corrupt according to the deceitful lusts, and be renewed in the spirit of your mind, and that you put on the new man which was created according to God, in true righteousness and holiness. Ephesians 4:22-24

The old man must yield place to the new man just as old orders change and yield place to the new. The former ways become incompatible with the new ways of life. Both could not co-exist.

Do not lie to one another, since you have put off the old man with his deeds, and have put on the new man who is renewed in knowledge according to the image of Him who created him Colossians 3:9, 10

h. We should live a new life in Christ

Paul reminds us that if we have become dead to sin through baptism, we are like dead people who are no longer bound by sin. And, as Christ was raised from the dead, we, too, should bury the "old man" and live a new life in Christ.

Therefore we were buried with him through baptism into death, that just as Christ was raised from the dead by the glory of the Father, even so we also should walk in newness of life Romans 6:4

i. Old creation will be forgotten when new ones are created

Writing on glorious creation, Isaiah said:

For behold, I create new heavens and a new earth; and the former shall not be remembered or come to mind Isaiah 65:17

According to the revelation of Jesus to John the beloved, all things will be made new:

Then He who sat on the throne said; "Behold I make all things new" and He said to me: Write, for these words are true and faithful. Revelation 21:5

The revelation of Christ for a new heaven and a new earth is creative (Rev. 21:12); an improvement on the present (Rev. 21:3) and offers a permanent solution (Rev. 21:6). Vision is an informed bridge to a better tomorrow. Jesus restores what we lost in the Garden of Eden.

j.   Lesson from the eagle

The eagle sheds its old feathers to grow new ones. This is what makes it renewed in strength and the secret of its soaring power. Like the eagle, we need to constantly shed our old "feathers" and grow new spiritual feathers so that we can soar higher and run faster. There are some old sinful habits we need to "lay aside" so that we may run this race successfully (Heb. 13: 1-2). Isaiah writes

But those who wait on the Lord shall renew their strength. They shall mount up with wings like eagles, they shall run and not be weary, they shall walk and not faint Isaiah 40:31

He satisfies our mouth with good things so that our youth is renewed like eagles (Psalm 103:5). This is one of the redemptive benefits we receive as Christians, which should not be taken for granted (Psalm 103:1-5)

Chapter 6

NEW WINE

Ordinarily, wine is viewed negatively as something intoxicating, an alcoholic beverage that is totally incompatible with Christian holiness or morality. Those who are given to wine usually lack self control, make poor judgments and cannot be entrusted with leadership positions: "They are out of the way through strong drink; they err in vision, they stumble in judgment" (Isa. 28:7).

Wine has caused great men to fall into sin and lose their sense of morality; Examples include Noah (Gen. 9: 20-24) and Lot (Gen. 19:32-38).

Wine is forbidden for men called into sacred office or anointed for Divine service. Abstinence from wine was required for priests (Lev. 10: 8-9), Nazarenes (Number 6:2-13) and anointed kings (Prov. 31:4-5).

Wine is a mocker, strong drink is raging: and whosoever is deceived thereby is not wise Prov. 20:1 KJV

The New Testament upholds a similar high moral standard in relation to wine; Church official – Bishops, Pastors, Elders, Deacons or Deaconesses – and all church workers must abstain from alcoholic beverages (1 Tim. 3:3, 8; Tit. 1:7; 2:3).

In his epistle to the church in Ephesus, Paul wrote:

And so do not be drunk with wine, in which is dissipation; but be filled with the Spirit Ephesians 5:18

Different Kinds of Wine

A close study of the bible, however, shows that "wine" is not always used in a negative sense for "strong drink" or alcoholic beverages. It is also used for fresh, grape juice, not the fermented wine (which is intoxicating) and the unfermented wine (which is pure, freshly pressed grape juice and is non-alcoholic).

In the Old Testament, the two Hebrew words used for wine are yayin and tirosh. The former, yayin, is used for wine – fermented, intoxicating wine. This was the wine that made Noah drunk (Gen. 9:21), the type of wine Lot's daughters gave him before they had incest with their father (Gen. 19:33-37). Priests were forbidden to drink wine on duty (Lev. 10:9). The latter, tirosh, refers to fresh grape juice – as freshly squeezed out. It is commonly used for fresh, sweet or new wine – in its unfermented state. This is like our "apple juice, "orange juice", "pineapple juice" or "grape juice" of today.

The most commonly used word in the New Testament is oions – that is, wine. When fermented, it becomes intoxicant and can cause an old wineskin to burst (Matt. 9:17). The miracle wine made by Jesus was oinos - fresh, sweet, grape juice – not intoxicating (See: John 2:1-11). In the institution of the Lord's Supper, Jesus refers to the content of the cup as "the fruit of the vine" (Matt. 26:29; Mark 14:25). This is why we use non-alcoholic beverage, any fruit juice that is red in colour, as emblem of the Blood of Jesus, in the Lord's Supper.

The Greek word "gleukos" is used only in Acts 2:13, where the accusers of the disciples said, "These men are full of new wine". It is used for sweet or new wine – fresh grape juice, before fermentation is complete. But it can become highly intoxicating, causing men to get drunk, when it has undergone a fermentation process. This was what the accusers thought when they heard the disciples speaking in foreign tongues and referred to them as: "They are just drunk, that's all" (NLT)

Wine as a Symbolism

Generally in the Bible, wine – fermented or unfermented – is used metaphorically; perhaps because of its strong influence on men, wine is used figuratively to represent certain actions, attitudes, virtues or vices, character or behaviour.   In this sense, wine is used positively for:

a.   Wisdom

Wisdom is the ability to judge correctly and to follow the best course of action, based on knowledge and understanding. According to Solomon, wisdom makes the difference, and, writing on the way of wisdom, he said:

Wisdom has built her house, she has hewn out her seven pillars, she has slaughtered her meat, she has mixed her wine, she has also furnished her table... Come, eat of bread and drink of wine I have mixed Proverbs 9: 1-2, 5

b.   Love

King Solomon writes:

Let him kiss me with the kisses of his mouth, for your love is better than wine Songs of Solomon 1:2

How fair is your love, my sister, my spouse! How much better than wine is your love, and the scent of perfume, than all spices! Song of Solomon 4:10.

c.   Wealth

"Come and buy wine and milk without money and without price..." (Isa. 55:1, 2); you need money to "buy wine". But the "wine" Jesus provides is priceless – without price, without money.

d.   Abundant Blessing

If we ever need God to increase our possessions we must honour Him with our estate. This abundant blessing is referred to as new wine which is divine reward for our liberal giving.

Solomon writes:

Honour the Lord with your possessions, and with the first fruits of all your increase; so your barns will be filled with plenty and your vats will overflow with new wine. Proverbs 3: 9, 10

New wine was also used metaphorically for abundant blessing by Prophet Joel when God spoke through him on refreshing the land of Judah. "The threshing floors shall be full of wheat, and the vats shall overflow with new wine and oil" (Joel 2:24). "And it will come to pass in that day that the mountains shall drip with new wine" (Joel 3:18).

Speaking on the restoration of Israel, Prophet Amos used the same metaphor.

"Behold, the days are coming," says the Lord, when the plowman shall overtake the reaper and the trader of grapes him who sows seed, the mountain shall drop with sweet wine, and the hills shall flow with it. Amos 9:13

Chapter 7

FRESH OIL

One of the essential elements of "new things" is fresh oil or new oil. Fresh oil looks fresh, smells fresh, tastes fresh and produces fresh results. We need fresh oil for fresh experiences, fresh breakthroughs and fresh exploits. It is needed for fresh revelation, new vision, fresh anointing, new strength to overcome new challenges and new zeal to accomplish new, bigger and better things in life, ministry, business and relationship.

Fresh oil is described as fresh oil (Num. 11:8; Psa. 92:10), pure oil (Exod. 27:20), precious oil (Psa. 133:2), golden oil (Zech 4:12), excellent oil (Psa. 141:5), new Spirit (Ezek. 18:31; 36:26) or new anointing. Fresh oil can open new doors into new blessings, new possibilities and usher you into a higher level of grace and unction in ministry.

This fresh oil is the oil of gladness with which Jesus was anointed more than anyone else (Psa. 45:7; Heb 1:9). It is also the Spirit of joy or of praise which is different from the spirit of mourning and heaviness – products of "old oil". Fresh oil is the fresh anointing which brings good news to the poor, comfort to the broken hearted and frees prisoners.

Prophet Isaiah declares:

The Spirit of the Lord is upon Me, because the Lord has anointed Me to preach good tidings to the poor; He has sent Me to heal the brokenhearted, to proclaim liberty to the captives, and the opening of the prison to those who are bound Isaiah 61:1

In verse 3, he says:

To console those who mourn in Zion, to give them beauty for ashes, the oil of joy for mourning, the garment of praise for the spirit of heaviness; that they may be called trees of righteousness; the planting of the Lord, that He may be glorified Isaiah 61:3

Naturally, oil serves several purposes; it is used for cooking, for lamps – to keep the lamp burning – for heat, to keep us warm when it is cold. It is used for the body, to preserve the natural beauty and texture of the skin; thus, it preserves against brittle and premature aging.

Solomon admonished: "Let your garment always be white, and let your head lack no oil" (Eccl. 9:8).

Oil makes the hair grow strong and keeps it against fragility. Also, it makes one's face to shine.

And wine that makes glad the heart of man, oil to make his face shine Psalm 104:15

When your face shines, every area of your life can glow with light. It can make your countenance cheerful and attractive. A shining face is a reflection of inward joy, a joyful spirit.

A merry heart makes a cheerful countenance, but by the sorrow of the heart the spirit is broken Proverbs 15:13

And, according to Solomon, a cheerful heart is good medicine

A merry heart does good, like medicine, but a broken spirit dries the bone Proverbs 17:22

Jesus had admonished us, when we fast to anoint our heads with oil and wash our faces. Thus, we will not appear mournful, melancholic or pitiable, like the hypocritical Pharisees in the bible.

Moreover when you fast, do not be like the hypocrites, with a sad countenance. For they disfigure their faces that they may appear to men to be fasting. Assuredly, I say to you, they have their reward. But you, when you fast, anoint your head and wash your face Matthew 6:16, 17

One good thing about oil, is that it is medicinal; it has inherent medicinal properties. The Good Samaritan applied oil on the wound of the man beaten by thieves on Jericho Road.

But a certain Samaritan, as he journeyed, came where he was. And when he saw him, he had compassion so he went to him, and bandaged his wound, pouring on oil and wine; and set him on his own animal, brought him to an inn, and took care of him Luke 10:33, 34

In a spiritual sense, oil or ointment serves as the balm that soothes the pains and heals the wounds and hurts of God's afflicted children; there is a 'Balm in Gilead'. Jesus is the Provider of that Balm; He is the Great Healer (Exod. 15:26), the Great Physician, who heals all our diseases (Psalm 103:2; Isaiah 53:5).

Is there no balm in Gilead, is there no physician there? Why then is there no recovery for the health of the daughter of my people? Jeremiah 8:22

As a symbol of the Holy Spirit, oil is used to convey healing power to the sick in addition to the prayer of faith.

Is anyone among you sick? Let him call for the elders of the church, and let them pray over him, anointing him with oil in the name of the Lord and the prayer of faith will save the sick, and the Lord will raise him up and if he has committed sins, he will be forgiven James 5:14, 15

In Pentecostal liturgy, 'anointing with oil' is a common practice. We usually use oil to anoint the sick; oil is used as a remedy and for the cure of sickness.

And He cast out many demons, and anointed with oil many who were sick, and healed them. Mark 6:13

In mechanical works, oil is used as a coolant and for lubrication. It lessens friction, reduces heat and makes things go smoothly. Some tough bolts and nuts that are hard to loosen can easily be untied when oil is applied. This can be applied figuratively to spiritual realities. As an emblem of the Holy Spirit, "anointing oil" can break spiritual yokes and loosen those that are spiritually tied by their enemies.

It shall come to pass in the day that his burden will he take away from your shoulder, and his yoke from your neck, and the yoke will be destroyed because of the anointing oil Isaiah 10:27

Why Fresh Oil?

It is not enough to use any oil; the oil must be pure, fresh, new, clean and unadulterated.

Only fresh, new oil can produce fresh and effective results. Old, used over, polluted or adulterated oil can be counterproductive; it can disappoint, back fire and work against you. So, you must always strive for fresh oil – oil for excellence.

Polluted oil makes food to become sour and perfume to stink. Solomon says that dead flies can cause a bottle of perfume to stink.

Dead flies cause the ointment of the apothecary to send forth a stinking savour so doth a little folly, him that is in reputation for wisdom and honour
Ecclesiastes 10:1

According to Solomon, a foreign body can cause "the ointment of the apothecary" to stink. The word "apothecary" is an archaic word for a druggist, pharmaceutical chemist. An apothecary was one who prepared and sold medicinal and cosmetic compounds. A dead fly in the ointment can negate the purpose of the medicine. It can render the ointment poisonous; thus, what was prepared to cure can cause harm.

Pure Oil For Lamps

In the Mosaic Era, the altar lamp of the Tabernacle was constantly filled with pure, fresh oil, and kept continuously burning.

***And you shall command the children of
Israel that they bring you pure oil of
pressed olives for the light, to cause the
lamp to burn continually*** Exodus 27:20

The olive oil to be used for the lamp must be
"pure" – fresh, new, unused before, "pure
olives oil". The Hebrew word used here for
"pure", is zak, which means clear, clean, pure.
It is from the word zakah, which denotes to be
translucent, to be innocent, to be clear, clean
or to be kept pure.

This "pure oil" was made of the finest quality.
It was made from beaten unripe olive and
crushed in the mortar without the application
of fire. The pulpy mass was then placed in a
clean cloth basket, where the oil was filtered
as pure, clear, clean and fresh oil.

This pure oil causes the lamp to burn with pure
light, smoothly, calmly and innocently, without
smoke or unpleasant odour. But this is not the
case with "old oil"; over used oil in the lamp
can cause health hazard in the house.

Spiritually, "anointing oil" that we carry in our
vessels must be clean, pure and kept fresh
always. The anointing in you must not be
polluted, contaminated or adulterated. You
should constantly seek to keep it pure, holy
and fresh, so that you can experience pure and
fresh breakthroughs. Those who carry God's
anointing must be pure.

***Depart! Depart! Go out from there, touch
no unclean thing; go out of the midst of
her, be clean; you who bear the vessels of
the Lord*** Isaiah 52:11

Writing to his spiritual son, Timothy, on the
need for leaders to be pure, Paul said: "But in
great house there are not only vessels of gold
and silver, but also of wood and clay, some for
honour and some for dishonour. Therefore if
anyone cleanses himself from the latter, he will
be a vessel to honour, sanctified and useful for
the Master, prepared for every good work" (2
Timothy 2:20, 21)

Saul was anointed by Prophet Samuel

***Then Samuel took a flask of oil and
poured it on his head, and kissed him and
said: Is it not because the Lord has
anointed you commander over his
inheritance?*** 1 Samuel 10:1

Again, we are told:

***So it was, when he had turned his back to
go from Samuel, that God gave him
another heart; and all those signs came to
pass that day. When they came there to
the hill there was a group of prophets to
meet him; then the Spirit of God came
upon him, and prophesied among them.
And it happened, when all who knew him***

formerly saw that he indeed prophesied among the prophets, that the people said to one another; what is this that has come upon the son of Kish? Is Saul also among the prophets? Then a man from there answered and said, "but who is their father"? Therefore it became a proverb; "Is Saul also among the prophets"? I Samuel 10:9-12

As Saul became more powerful, he increasingly became proud, arrogant and independent of God. Consequently, God "rejected" Saul (1 Sam. 15:23, 26).

Saul's anointing became "mixed" and polluted, and he sometimes behaved like a "mad man". An evil spirit which mixed with his anointing constantly tormented him (1 Sam. 16:14-23).

At last, when Saul could no longer hear from God, he secretly sought for help from a witch – the witch of Endor.

When Saul saw the army of the Philistines, he was afraid, and his heart trembled greatly. And when Saul inquired of the Lord, and the Lord did not answer him, either by dreams or by the prophets. Then Saul said to his servants, "find me a woman who is a medium, that I may go to her and inquire of her" And his servants said to him; "in fact there is a woman who is a medium at Endor". 1 Samuel 28:5-7

Finally, Saul's mixed anointing disappointed and disgraced him; he committed suicide in the battle between Israel and the Philistines.

We are told:

Then said Saul to his armour bearer; "Draw your sword, and thrust me through with it, lest these uncircumcised men come and thrust me through and abuse me." But the armour bearer would not... Saul took a sword and fell on it. And when his armour bearer saw that Saul was dead, he also fell on his sword, and died with him. So Saul, his three sons, his armour bearer and his men died together that same day. 1 Samuel 31:4-6

Beloved, my prayer for you is that you will not end as Saul did. I admonish you to constantly keep the oil in your vessel clean, pure and fresh. Do not corrupt or adulterate or commercialize this oil. Keep your vessel clean, keep your oil fresh all the time and keep away from those who operate with "mixed anointing" or counterfeit oil.

Fresh Oil For New Exploits

Fresh oil is necessary to keep you fresh, constantly relevant and prepared for new exploits and assignments. The oil of last year will not meet the needs and challenges of the New Year; you need new oil for new exploits.

Those who depend on past used oil, will not be relevant for tomorrow's challenges.

Some of us are ineffective in our present levels of ministry, because we are still operating with the same old oil, which has lost its worth and usefulness. You need to change your oil so that your spiritual engine can run faster, smoother and cooler. Old oil can dry up and cause your 'engine to knock'; thus you become useless and incapacitated.

But my horn You have exalted like a wild ox; I have been anointed with fresh oil Psalm 92:10

In the New Living Translation, "fresh oil" is translated "finest oil". Fresh oil or finest oil can renew your spiritual engine, for excellence in ministry and supernatural exploits in warfare. The fresher or finer your oil, the greater will be your exploits, the faster and farther you will run and the higher you will soar and excel.

Samson: A Case Study

The life of Samson exemplifies a minister who operates with fresh oil and old oil; Samson experienced both. When his anointing was fresh, innocent and pure, Samson was the strongest of men – stronger than the strongest giant in the ancient world. He could rip a lion apart with his bare hands; he could do so as easily as though it were a young goat.

So Samson went down to Timnah with his father and mother, and came to the vineyards of Timnah. Now to his surprise, a young lion came roaring against him. And the spirit of the Lord came mightily upon him, and he tore the lion apart as one would have torn apart a young goat, though he had nothing in his hand. But he did not tell his father or his mother what he had done. Judges 14:5,6

On another occasion – when Samson's oil was still fresh – he was so powerfully anointed that he slew 1000 armed Philistines who came to capture him; he killed them with a new jawbone of a donkey. The fresh anointing upon him was like fire, it burnt the rope with which he was tied.

When he came to Lehi, the Philistines came shouting against him. Then the Spirit of the Lord came mightily upon him; and ropes that were on his arms became like flax that is burned with fire, and his bonds broke loose from his hands. He found a fresh jawbone of a donkey, reached out his hand and took it, and killed a thousand men with it. Then Samson said: "With the jawbone of a donkey, heaps upon heaps, with the

jawbone of a donkey I have slain a thousand" 1 Samuel 15:14-16

But when Samson began to be complacent, living in sin, his oil became sour, impure, adulterated and weaker. Instead of seeking to renew his oil, he became presumptuous, proud and careless, living on past glory and exploits – totally, dependent on his old oil. This old oil soon ran out, making him dry, empty and powerless; yet he remained presumptuous.

When the same Philistines – the enemies he had defeated in the past – came to capture him, Samson presumed that he could "shake himself" and go out as he did before; but he did not realize that God had left him.

And she said: "The Philistines are upon you, Samson!" So he awoke from his sleep, and said; I will go out as before, at other times, and shake myself free!" But he did not know that the Lord had departed from him. Then the Philistines took him and put out his eyes, and brought him down to Gaza. They bound him with bronze fetters, and he became a grinder in the prisons Judges 16:20, 21

Notice his presumptuous attitude: "I will go out as at other times and shake myself" (Judges 16:20 KJV) or "I will do as before and shake myself" (NLT). But he did not realize that God had departed from him.

You cannot continue doing ministry as before –
as you did in the past, with the same old oil.
You need to change your oil, seek to be filled
and full with fresh oil – fresh unction, fresh
anointing – so that you can burn with fresh
fires, do fresh exploits, explore new territories
and overcome new challenges; thus you can
mount up to new heights.

Your old oil has served its purpose and time;
now you need to go forward and soar higher.
You need fresh fuel, fresh oil, to accomplish
your new assignment. There is still a lot to
accomplish; you need that oil of gladness to
excel. It is the same oil with which Christ
Himself was anointed above His fellows (Heb.
1:9); the oil of joy which makes the face to
shine instead of mourning which disfigures the
countenance and makes it unlovely. The oil
will beautify you, energise and inspire you to
accomplish beyond your natural capacity. You
will encounter the joy unspeakable and full of
glory and who ever encounters the joy of God
must have the praise and glory.

Chapter 8

SEASON OF NEW SONGS

Singing plays a prominent part in our lives and, especially, our culture and religion. Among the Hebrews, singing was very prominent in their worship and national life. It was not uncommon for the Jews to compose a song to celebrate some victories or a significant religious experience. For example, Moses composed a song of deliverance and praise, after God led Israel out of Egypt and divided the Red Sea; Miriam joined in the singing, too.

Then Moses and the children of Israel sang this song to the Lord, and spoke; saying: "I will sing to the Lord, for He has triumphed gloriously! The horse and its rider He has thrown into the sea! The Lord is my strength and song, and He has become my God, and I will praise Him. The Lord is a man of war; the Lord is His name" Exodus 15:1-3

Then Miriam the prophetess, the sister of Aaron, took the timbrel in her hand; and all the women went out after her with timbrels and with dance. And Miriam answered them: "Sing to the Lord, for He has triumphed gloriously! The horse and its rider He has thrown into the sea". Exodus 15:20, 21

Deborah and Barak composed a song of praise, thanking God for Israel's victory over King Jabin's army at Mount Tabor.

Then Deborah and Barak the son of Abinoam sang on that day, saying: "When leaders lead in Israel, when the people willingly offered themselves, bless the Lord! Hear O king! Give ear O princes! I even I, will sing unto the Lord; I will sing praise to the Lord God of Israel. Judges 5: 1-3

In Africa – like in Jewish culture – singing is part of our culture. We sing to communicate and to express our feelings or emotions, depending on our mood, the occasion or circumstance or the season. We have different kinds of song for different occasions; we sing during wedding, when a new baby is born, when we bury the dead, when we experience victory in battle, when a miracle happens or when we celebrate a significant breakthrough.

As Christians, however, in all our singing, we must reflect Christian culture and the goodness of God. We sing because God is good, and that, in His goodness He has given us something worthy of celebration. According to Apostle James, "Are any of you happy? You should sing praises" (James 5:13 NLT). Apostle Paul admonished Christians to sing psalms and spiritual songs, with Christian music to the Lord.

Speaking to one another in psalms and hymns and spiritual songs, singing and making melody in your heart to the Lord Ephesians 5:19

David was a great singer and composer; he usually sang joyfully and purposefully to express his gratitude to God for special victories and breakthroughs.

He said:

I will sing to the Lord, because He has dealt bountifully with me Psalms 13:6

He delivers me from my enemies, You also lift me up above those who rise against me; You have delivered me from the violent man. Therefore I will give thanks to You, O Lord among the Gentiles, and sing praise to your name Psalm 18:48, 49

Again, he said:

And now my head shall be lifted up above my enemies all around me; Therefore I will offer sacrifice of joy in His tabernacle, I will sing, yes, I will sing praises to the Lord Psalm 27:6

It is difficult to sing a joyful song when we are in bitterness or in a sorrowful mood. This was the experience of the Jews in the land of captivity.

By the rivers of Babylon, there we sat down, yea we wept when we remembered Zion. We hung our harps upon the willow in the midst of it. For there, those who carried us away captive asked of us a song, and those who plundered us requested mirth, saying, "sing us one of the songs of Zion". How shall we sing the Lord's song in a foreign land? Psalm 137: 1-4

God can deliver you from your captivity and put a new song in your mouth. You can sing joyful songs again, when the Lord turns your captivity and restores your joy. He can fill your mouth with laughter and give you a new voice, to sing a new song.

When the Lord brought back the captivity of Zion, we were like those who dream. Then our mouth was filled with laughter, and our tongue with singing, then they said among the nations, the Lord has done great things for us, and we are glad. Psalm 126:1-3

Time To Sing Again

It is time to sing a new song when your tough times are over and gone and when light shines in your darkness, your worst "winter" and the heavy rains that hindered your song are now over and gone. Your season of singing has now come. The sun is shining again, bitter things are becoming better things and your "night" has turned to "morning" (Psa. 30:5). Your life will witness a turn around because God is ready to re-write your story. Prepare your voice to sing new songs:

Now you can join Solomon to sing:

For lo, the winter is past; the rain is over and gone. The glower appears on the earth; the time of singing has come. And the voice of the turtledove is heard in our land Song of Solomon 2:11, 12

Time For A new Song

A new song is to be clearly distinguished from old songs. Old songs are the "same old song," of the past, songs that reflect past failures and negativities; songs of barrenness, poverty, dryness, bitterness, sorrow, mourning, reproach or curses. But a new song overshadows all your old songs; it is a song of joy , victory, bountiful harvest, positive testimonies, progress, great exploits, healing, uncommon miracles, supernatural breakthroughs and celebration of new, positive experiences.

David said:

You have turned for me my mourning into dancing; You have put off my sackcloth and clothed me with gladness. To the end that my glory may sing praise to You and not be silent. O Lord my God, I will give thanks to You forever Psalm 30:11, 12

A New Song For The Barren

Barrenness is desolation, emptiness, unproductivity, dryness, sterility, fruitlessness or unprofitability.

One can be barren in marriage, in ministry, in business and, even, in the work of God. There is a song for barrenness – song of reproach (Gen. 30:23; Luke 1:25) – and there is a new song which replaces the former, when this reproach is rolled away. This is my prayer for you, that God will remove the reproach and song of barrenness from your life, and give you a new song, a song of fruitfulness.

David said:

He grants the barren woman a home like a joyful mother of children, praise the Lord Psalm 113:9

According to David, God can change your barren condition and make you a happy mother of many children. He has done it before; He has done it for many, and He can, and will, do it for you, too. Thus, you can sing, "Praise Ye The LORD", that is, "Hallelujah Song" – a song of praise and victory.

The Lord has given this word of hope, comfort and assurance, through Prophet Isaiah:

"Sing O barren, you who have not borne! Break forth into singing, and cry aloud, you who have not laboured with child! For more are the children of the desolate than the children of the married woman" says the Lord. Enlarge the place of your tent, and let them stretch out the curtains of your dwellings, do not spare, lengthen your cords and strengthen your stakes. For you shall expand to the right and to the left, and your descendants will inherit the nations. And make the desolate cities inhabited. Isaiah 54:1-3

A change of story brings a change in your singing; when an old story becomes a new story, a new song follows. There are several examples of women whose songs changed, when their stories changed. Instead of their old songs of reproach, they sang the "Hallelujah song" – a new song of praise, victory and joy.

Sarah:

Before her story changed, she sang the song of doubt, unbelief, self pity, reproach and hopelessness. (Gen.18:11-14).

But after the Lord visited her and blessed her with a son, her song changed; she sang a new song. Those who had laughed at her, when they heard her story, came to laugh with her.

And Sarah said; "God has made me laugh, and all who hear will laugh with me". She also said: "Who would have said to Abraham that Sarah would nurse children? For I have borne him a son in his old age" Genesis 21: 6, 7

Hannah:

Hannah's old story is described as follows:

And her rival provoked her severely, to make her miserable, because the Lord has closed her womb. So it was, year by year, when she went up to the house of the Lord, that she provoked her: therefore she wept and did not eat. Then Elkanah, her husband said to her; "Hannah, why do you weep? Why do you not eat? Am I not better to you than ten sons?" 1 Samuel 1:6-8

Her old song was a song of tears, bitterness, reproach and of sorrow; for "she was in bitterness of soul… and wept sore" and "a woman of a sorrowful spirit" (1 Samuel 1: 9, 15).

But when Hannah's miracle happened, her song changed; her song was new, loud, powerful and positive. It was a song of joy and dancing, with positive testimonies.

Hannah prayed and said:

"My heart rejoices in the Lord; my horn is exalted in the Lord, I smile at my enemies, because I rejoice in Your salvation. No one is holy like the Lord, for there is none besides You, nor is there any rock like our God. Talk no more so very proudly; let no arrogance come from your mouth, for the Lord is the God of knowledge, and by Him actions are weighed. The bows of the mighty men were broken, and those who stumbled are girded with strength. Those who were full have hired themselves out for bread, and the hungry have ceased to hunger, even the barren has borne seven, and she who has many children has become feeble
1 Samuel 2:1-5

Let us take note of verse 5, where she said, "the barren hath born seven" or "the childless woman now has seven". She must have spoken prophetically and by faith when she made that declaration; for she was blessed with more children after Samuel was born.

And the Lord visited Hannah, so that she conceived and bore three sons and two daughters. Meanwhile the child Samuel grew before the Lord 1 Samuel 2:21

I pray that the Lord who is a Repeat Performer will remember you as He remembered Hannah and remove old songs of reproach, sorrow and bitterness from your life and put new songs of testimonies, joy and dancing in your mouth.

The Widow of Nain

The story of the poor widow of Nain presents a positive testimony of a changed story and a new song. Her "funeral song" turned to a celebration when Jesus raised her son from death. She was on her way to the village cemetery, followed by a funeral procession – a procession of mourners, singing "funeral hymns".

Now it happened, the day after, that He went into a city called Nain, many of His disciples went with Him, and a large crowd. And when He came near the gate of the city, behold, a dead man was being carried out, the only son of his mother; and she was a widow. And a large crowd from the city was with her Luke 7:11, 12

As they were approaching the gate of the village, Jesus met her and comforted her. He touched the coffin and the bearers stopped. Jesus then commanded the dead boy to rise up; the boy immediately arose, he sat up and began to talk.

When the Lord saw her, he had compassion on her and said to her, "do not weep". Then He came and touched the open coffin, and those who carried him stood still. And He said, "young man, I say unto you arise". So he who was dead sat up and began to speak. And He presented him to his mother Luke 7:13 -15

Consequently, the "funeral song" changed to a celebration. We are told that "They glorified God" or "They praised God". That is, they sang a new song, the "Hallelujah" song.

And fear came upon all, and they glorified God, saying "A great prophet has risen up among us and God has visited His people". Luke 7:16

I pray that you will encounter the visitation of God as you are reading this book. The Lord will wipe away tears from your eyes; those who witnessed your sorrow will witness your turn around and celebrate with you.

David's New Song

David usually sang new songs and urged others to do the same. He had good reasons to celebrate each victory with a new song of praise to God.

In Psalm 33:1 – 3, he says:

Rejoice in the Lord, O you righteous! For praise from the upright is beautiful. Praise the Lord with the harp, make melody to Him with an instrument of ten strings. Sing to Him a new song, play skillfully with a shout of joy.

Again, he says:

O sing to the Lord a new song for He has done marvelous things; His right and His holy arm have gained Him the Victory Psalm 98:1

I will sing a new song to You, O God; on a harp of ten strings I will sing praises to You. The One who gives salvation to kings, who delivered David His servant from the deadly sword. Psalm 144:9, 10

In Psalm 40, after waiting patiently on God in prayer, his breakthrough came. He said:

I waited patiently for the Lord, and He inclined to me and heard my cry. He also brought me up out of a horrible pit, out of the miry clay, and set my feet upon a rock, and established my steps Psalm 40: 1, 2

First, God heard his cry and answered his prayer. Secondly, God lifted him out of the pit of despair. Thirdly, God set his feet on solid ground. Fourthly, God established him and steadied him as he walked. And finally, God put a new song in his mouth

And he hath put a new song in my mouth, even praise unto our God: many shall see it, and fear, and shall trusting the LORD Psalm 40:3

What a mighty God we serve! From one extreme negativity of sinking in miry clay, to another extreme of positivity, he was set on a rock. I pray that all your negativities will be turned to positivities and the Lord will put a new song in your mouth in the name of JESUS.

I close this chapter with this prophetic prayer for you: that God will give you victory on every front, over household enemy, financial setback, rejection, ill-health and failure at the point of success; that the God of new beginnings will raise you from minimum to maximum in your life, family, business and in your ministry. At every stage of your victory, God will put new songs in your mouth.

This is your season of new songs and celebration, and joyful songs will be your testimony.

Chapter 9

A NEW HEART FOR NEW THINGS

The place of the heart in life, relationship and Christian service cannot be overemphasized. The heart is the center of life, religion and ministry. Everything we do in life, ministry and relationship springs from the heart. Our words, actions, feelings and decisions reflect the state of our heart.

Jesus said:

A good man out of the good treasure of his heart brings forth good; and an evil man out of the evil treasure of his heart brings forth evil. For out of the abundance of the heart his mouth speaks Luke 6: 45.

According to Jesus, the heart is the center of life. Moreover, it can be said that the heart:

a. Determines character

The heart says much about who you are, your action, reaction and your character. The heart is the seat of the conscience (Heb. 10:22).

Solomon writes: "For as he thinks in his heart so is he..." (Prov. 23:7). Your character paints the picture of your personality and, like smoke, no matter how you pretend to cover up your character, it will come out to reveal and expose the hidden things about the real you.

b.   Is the source of evil

The heart is the centre of physical life and also the centre of mental and spiritual life. It is the inner man, it keeps secrets and is unsearchable (Psalm 44:21). As the mental centre, the heart knows (Deut 29:4), understands (Isa. 44:18) and remembers (Isa. 42: 25). It is the engine room of all evil plans. A man may have evil heart (Prov. 26:23), be godless in heart (Job 36:13), or deceitful in heart (Jer. 17:3).

Jesus said:

But those things which proceed out of the mouth come from the heart, and they defile a man. For out of the heart proceed evil thoughts, murders, adulteries, fornications, thefts, false witness, blasphemies. These are the things which defile a man, but to eat with unwashed hands does not defile a man   Matthew 16:18-20

c.   Is the source of speech

The heart is the emotional centre. It is the seat of joy (Isa. 65:14), courage (Psa. 27:14), pain (Prov. 25:10), anxiety (Prov. 12:25), despair (Eccl. 2:20), sorrow (Neh. 2:2) and fear (Deut. 28:28). Out of the abundance of the heart, the mouth speaks (Matt. 12:34). Words spoken from the heart carry a thought that shapes or destroys a destiny. Words transmit power (Matt.12:33-37); words determine our reward and judgment (Matt. 12:36, 37). Words produce fruits (Matt. 12: 33, 35, 36); words shape our destiny (Matt. 12:37).

d.   Is the source of faith

The heart is the dwelling place of the spirit and the Lord (2 Cor. 1:22; Eph. 3:17); the heart receives the love and peace of God (Rom. 5:5; Col. 3:15); the heart is the moral centre: God tries the heart (Psa. 17:3; Jer. 12:3), sees the heart (Jer. 20:12) and refines the heart (Psa. 26:2).

Explaining law of salvation, what to do to be saved, Paul said: "that if you confess with your mouth the Lord Jesus and believe in your heart that God raised Him from the dead, you will be saved" (Rom. 10:9).

Paul concluded:

For with the heart one believes unto righteousness, and with the mouth confession is made unto salvation
Romans 10:10

To a large extent, the heart dictates the way we live, and influences our feelings and desires. Solomon advises us to guard our hearts above everything else. We should discipline its desires and set boundaries where feelings are concerned.

Keep your heart with all diligence for out of it spring the issues of life Proverbs 4:23

Jonathan Edward said:

The first and great work of a Christian is about his heart. Do not be content with seeking to do good in "outward acts" while your heart is bad, and you are a stranger to the greater internal heart duties 7

The Human Heart

The heart is a hollow muscular organ that keeps up the circulation of blood by contracting and dilating. It is this consistent circulation of blood through the system that constitutes and sustains life. Thus, life ceases when the heart fails to circulate blood; "for the life of the flesh is in the blood" (Lev.17:11).

....
7. The New Encyclopedia of Christian Quotations, Hampshire: John Hunt Publishing Ltd., 2000, PP. 465, 466

The word is used figuratively in a variety of ways to describe our emotions, feelings, mood, desires and inward dispositions.

In this figurative sense, the "heart" is not the hollow physical organ, but the invisible, spiritual and sensitive organ which is responsible for our feelings, emotions and especially, love or hate. Appearance can be deceitful; it can present a false impression; only God can know the state of the heart

But the Lord said to Samuel; "Do not look at his appearance or at his physical stature, because I have refused him. For the Lord does not see as man sees, for man looks at the outward appearance, but the Lord looks at the heart 1 Samuel 16:7

The "physical heart" can be exchanged or transplanted, but the "spiritual heart" cannot be exchanged. If one had a heart transplant, he or she would still reflect his individuality – personality and character – and not that of the donor.

In the Old Testament, the two most frequently used Hebrew words are led and lebad; both are synonymous. Leb-derived from lebad – is used for the heart, the most internal organ. It is often used to mean the inner person, with a focus on the psychological aspects of the heart and mind.

It includes the human feelings, will, intellect and the ability to make decisions.

The Lord saw that the wickedness of man was great in the earth, and that every intent of the thoughts of his heart was only evil continually. And the Lord was sorry that He had made man on earth, and He was grieved in His heart Genesis 6:5-6

The word is also used for the physical hollow organ of the body. A complete victory was gained over Absalom's forces in his rebellion against his father, David. Joab killed Absalom by thrusting three spears through his heart.

Then Joab said; "I cannot linger with you". And he took three spears in his hand and thrust them through Absalom's heart while he was still alive in the midst of the terebinth tree. 2 Samuel 18:14

The "spiritual heart" is used of the inner man, the hidden man, that is, that part of man with which he thinks, lives, feels, loves, has a personality and, most importantly, is responsive towards God, His Word and His Will.

Moses urged the children of Israel to obey the simple command of God because they could not plead excuse of their disobedience on the ground of unintelligible, impracticable or impossible to be known or to be done. The Word of God was not hidden from them (Deut.

30:12); to enquire what they must do to please God, they did not need to go beyond the sea (Deut. 30:13).

Moses declared:

But the word is very near you, in your mouth and in your heart, that you may do it Deuteronomy 30:14

How can one be saved from God's just condemnation? Paul explains his answer in Romans 10:9: "that if you confess with your mouth the Lord Jesus and believe in your heart that God has raised Him from the dead, you will be saved".

In his call to repentance in his message to Judah, Joel wrote:

So rend your heart, and not your garments; return to the Lord your God, for He is gracious and merciful, slow to anger, and of great kindness; and He relents from doing harm. Who knows if He will turn and relent, and leave a blessing behind him – a grain offering and a drink offering for the Lord your God? Joel 2:13, 14

In seeking God we must search for Him with diligence and this will be with our hearts. We must continue seeking and take pains in seeking with sincerity, uprightness, vigour and fervency. Speaking through Jeremiah, God said:

And you will seek Me and find Me, when you search Me with all your heart Jeremiah 29:13

In the New Testament, the Greek word for "heart" is kardia; the English word "cardiac" (heart) comes from this Greek Word. It is used for "the heart" as the most important organ of the human body, the chief organ of physical life.

According to W. E. Vine:

By an easy translation the word came to stand for man's entire mental and moral activity, both the rational and emotional elements. In other words, the heart is used figuratively for the hidden springs of the personal life... The heart as lying deep within, contains 'the hidden man', (1 Pet. 3:4), the real man. It represents the true character but conceals it. 8

What Is A New Heart?

As it was previously discussed, a new heart is not a transplant or changing one's heart with another through medical surgery. If a wicked man's heart were to be replaced with the heart of "David" or "Abraham", he will never behave like David or Abraham; he will still behave normally in his old wicked ways.

A new heart is given by God; it is a divine act, a spiritual work, to become a "new man" or a "new creature".

A new heart is not received through medical surgery; it is received through "Divine surgery" – the supernatural "circumcision of the heart" by the Holy Spirit.

Paul explained in Romans 2 that the circumcision of the flesh is of no avail if it is not accompanied with the circumcision of the heart because we have been saved from the curse of the law. "But he is a Jew who is one inwardly; and circumcision is that of the heart, in spirit, not in the letter; whose praise is not from men but from God" (Rom. 2:29).

Writing on the blessing of returning to God, Moses said; "And the Lord your God will circumcise your heart and the heart of your descendants, to love the Lord your God with all your heart and with all your soul, that you may live" (Deut. 30:6)

A heart becomes "new", when God touches the "old heart" and replaces it with a fresh heart, making the person submissive and responsive to God.

....

8.   W. E. Vine, Vine's Expository Dictionary of New Testament Words, Massachusetts: Hendrickson Publishers, (no date), P. 546.

Speaking through Prophet Ezekiel, God said:

Then I will give them one heart, and I will put a new spirit within them, and take the stony out of their flesh, and give them a heart of flesh, that they may walk in my statutes and keep My judgments and do them, and they shall be My people, and I will be their God. Ezekiel 11:9, 20

Samuel said to Saul:

Then the Spirit of the Lord will come upon you, and you will prophesy with them and be turned into another man. And let it be, when these signs come to you, that you do as the occasion demands; for God is with you. 1 Samuel 10: 6, 7

We are told:

So it was, when he had turned his back to go from Samuel, that God gave him another heart; and all those signs came to pass that day 1 Samuel 10:9

The dramatic change people noticed in Saul after he received a "new heart" and became "another man" was made possible by a number of factors.

(i)   Samuel spoke words of revelation and inspiration which inspired Saul to overcome his fears and stepped out (1 Sam. 10:3-6).

(ii)   Saul opened his heart to God to operate upon – the inner man that connects us with the creator.

(iii)   What gave Saul the greatest satisfaction of all was that he found immediately that God had given him another heart. A new fire was kindled in his heart such as he had never before been acquainted with.   Seeking the asses was out of his heart; he thought about redressing the grievances of Israel, how to defeat the armies of the Philistines, administering justice and providing for public safety in Israel.

We are told:

When they came there to the hill, there was a group of prophets to meet him; then the spirit of God came upon him; and he prophesied among them. And it happened when all who knew him formerly saw that he indeed prophesied among the prophets, that the people said to one another: "What is this that has come upon the son of Kish? Is Saul also among the prophets?" Therefore it became a proverb. "Is Saul also among the prophets?   1 Samuel 10:10-12

God is in possession of the key to human heart. What He did for Saul, He will do for anybody who surrenders his or her soul to Him and seeks Him diligently with all his or her heart. From this day forward, I decree and declare: receive a new heart and become a new person in Jesus' name.

Why A New Heart?

The Divine promise of "a new thing" and the blessings contained in this promise cannot be experienced with an "old heart" – that is, the old, unbroken, carnal and stony heart. It takes a new heart to receive and experience God's "new things". A new heart gives you a new insight into the "new things" promised by God. It gives you a heart to desire new things, a fresh passion to seek for new things and a renewed inner strength to receive new things.

Paul said:

But is written: "Eye has not seen, nor ear heard, nor have entered into the heart of man the things which God has prepared for those who love Him". But God has revealed them to us through His spirit. For the spirit searches all things, yes, the deep things of God 1 Corinthians 2: 9, 10

A new heart is necessary to prepare you for your future blessings and ministry. Your "old heart" will always hinder your progress and keep you in the realm of past experiences. But a new heart will prepare you for the "new things" God has promised to give you; it will help you forget "the former things", so that you can focus on new blessings and confidently go forward to accomplish new things.

Whenever God intends to do new things for His people, He will give them a new heart – a circumcised heart, a Spirit touched heart from God. God gave Saul a new heart, and he became "another man" – different from the "old Saul" – to prepare him for his future role as king in Israel (1 Sam. 10: 6, 7, 9).

It takes a new heart to please God. The carnal heart cannot know God, cannot please God and cannot serve God. Only a renewed heart, through a renewed spirit, can do God's will, in God's own way.

Paul explains:

For those who live according to the flesh set their minds on the things of the flesh, but those who live according to the spirit, the things of the spirit. For to be carnally minded is death, but to be spiritually minded is life and peace. Because the carnal mind is enmity against God; for it is not subject to the law of God, nor indeed can be. So then, those who are in the flesh cannot please God Romans 8:5-8.

Paul wrote to the carnally minded Corinthians:

And I brethren, could not speak to you as to spiritual people but as to carnal, as to babes in Christ. I fed you with milk and not with solid food; but until now you were not able to receive it, and even now you are still not able, for you are still carnal. For where there are envy, strife, and divisions among you, are you not carnal and behaving like mere men? 1 Corinthians 3: 1-3

We can receive spiritual things when our hearts are renewed by the Spirit of God and in a right relationship with Him.

David, writing on the king of Glory, His Kingdom and who may ascend into the hill of the Lord and stand in His holy place, said:

He who has clean hands and pure heart, who has not lifted up his soul to an idol, nor sworn deceitfully. He shall receive blessing from the Lord, and righteousness from the God of his salvation Psalm 24: 4, 5

God has some great things in store for us, both of this life and of the future life. There are some "deep things of God" which He reveals by His Spirit, only to a regenerated heart.

Writing on spiritual wisdom, Paul said:

But it is written: "Eye has not seen, nor ear heard, nor have entered into the heart of man the things which God has prepared for those who love Him. But God has revealed them to us through His Spirit. For the spirit teaches all things, yes, the deep things of God. For what man knows the things of a man except the spirit of the man which is in him? Even so no one knows the things of God except the Spirit of God. Now we have received not the spirit of the world, but the spirit who is from God, that we might know the things which have been freely given to us by God. 1 Corinthians 2:9-12

Unregenerated hearts cannot comprehend spiritual truths, and cannot benefit from the blessings of the Spirit for the Church in this End Time. Only those who are spiritually minded – whose hearts have been renewed by God – can understand and respond to the demand of the Spirit.

But the natural man receives not the things of the spirit of God, for they are foolishness to him, nor can he know them, because they are spiritually discerned. But he who is spiritual judges all things, yet he himself is rightly judged by no one 1 Corinthians 2:14, 15

The "old", "unchanged" heart is depraved. It is desperately wicked, hardened and prone to evil.

Humankind had grown so evil that God was grieved in His heart for ever creating man.

Then the Lord saw the wickedness of man was great in the earth, and that every intent of the thoughts of his heart was only evil continually. And the Lord was sorry that He had made man on earth, and He was grieved in His heart Genesis 6:5,6

Similarly, Jeremiah, writing on Judah's sin and punishment, said: "The heart is deceitful above all things and desperately wicked; who can know it" (Jer. 17:9).

As depraved humans, we need a new heart to do what is right in the sight of God. And only God can change the heart; just like we cannot change the colour of our skin, and a leopard cannot remove its spots, so we cannot live righteously by our own power.

God, speaking through Jeremiah, said:

Can the Ethiopian change his skin or the leopard its spots? Then may you also do good who are accustomed to do evil Jeremiah 13:23

A new heart is necessary to receive God's Word. A new heart makes us spiritually receptive to His Word. And the Word grows and produces good fruits when it is sown in a renewed heart.

Speaking on the Proverb of the sower, Jesus said:

But others fell on good ground, sprang up, and yielded a crop a hundredfold, when He had said these things, He cried: "He who has ears to hear let him hear!" ...The ones that fell on good ground are those who, having heard the word with a noble and good heart, keep it and bear fruit with patience Luke 8: 8, 15

As Jesus interprets the current events to two grieving men who conversed about Jesus crucifixion, they struggled to understand what it all meant. Jesus saw their confusion that they needed someone to guide them. So He joined them on their journey to Emmaus and began to explain His resurrection in the light of scripture (Luke 24: 27, 45). By the end of their time together it all made sense and their heart burned within them.

And said to one another; "Did not our heart burn within us while He talked with us on the road, and while He opened the scriptures to us? Luke 24:32

It is only God that can open the heart of a sinner to receive the infallible word of God. God grants a sinner receptive heart to receive, understand and act on the word of God as spoken by the preacher.

This was what happened when Lydia got saved through the message of Paul.

Now a certain woman named Lydia heard us. She was a seller of purple from the city of Thyatira, who worshipped God. The Lord opened her heart to heed the things spoken by Paul Acts 16:14

Though the Preacher plants and another waters, the actual increase comes from the Lord. Neither the one who plants nor the one who waters is anything but God who grants the increase (1 Cor. 3:7).

Like Jeremiah, every leader experiences both good and bad days. Jeremiah chapter 20 allows us to see into the heart of a great prophet, Jeremiah, who complained to God and cursed the day he was born after praising God for his victories. Jeremiah found it very difficult to withdraw from the service of God much as he tried because God took control of his heart so that God's word in his heart was like a burning fire.

Then I said: "I will not make mention of Him, nor speak anymore in His name". But

His word was in my heart like a burning fire shut up in my bones; I was weary of holding it back, and I could not. Jeremiah 20:9

Paul gave this admonition:

And let the peace of God rule in your hearts, to the which also ye are called in one body; and be thankful. Let the word of Christ dwell in you richly in all wisdom, teaching and admonishing one another in psalms and hymns and spiritual songs, signing with grace in your hearts to the Lord Colossians 3:15-16 KJV

May your heart be circumcised that you may cling and be responsive to Him so that you may serve the Lord with a new zeal and a new spirit, Amen.

Chapter 10

DIVINE PROMISES AND CONDITIONS FOR A NEW HEART

In the previous chapter, our discussion was focused on the nature of a new heart; what a new heart is and why it is important. This chapter is a continuation from the previous discussion. Our focus will be on Divine promises for a new heart and how we can receive a new heart.

Divine Promise For A New Heart

God has not only promised to "do a new thing", He has also promised to give His people "a new heart" to receive new things and to serve Him with a new zeal, in a new way.

In the Old Testament, Jehovah promised to restore His people – both physically and spiritually. To accomplish this, He would give them a new heart and put a new spirit within them.

God spoke to His people, through Prophet Ezekiel, and promised to give them "one heart", put His Spirit within them and take away their stony, stubborn and rebellious heart – the "old heart" that had prevented them from doing God's will. In exchange, He will give them a tender, responsive and willing heart – "the heart of flesh".

God, speaking through Prophet Ezekiel on the restoration of Israel, said:

Then I will give them one heart, and I will put a new spirit within them, and take the stony heart out of their flesh, and give them a heart of flesh

Ezekiel 11:19

Ezekiel also wrote:

Then I will sprinkle clean water on you and you shall be clean, I will cleanse you from all filthiness and from all your idols. I will give you a new heart and put a new spirit within you; I will take the heart of stone out of your flesh and give you a heart of flesh Ezekiel 36:25, 26

With this new heart, God's people will obey God and His ordinances and positively walk in His precepts.

We are told:

That they may walk in My statutes and keep My judgments and do them; and they shall be My people and I will be their God Ezekiel 11:20

We are also told:

I will put My spirit within you and cause you to walk in My statutes, and you will

keep My judgments and do them   Ezekiel 36:27

Again, Jehovah gave this promise through Prophet Jeremiah:

Then I will give them heart to know Me that I am the Lord and they shall be My people, and I will be their God, for they shall return to Me with their whole heart Jeremiah 24:7

Jeremiah also wrote:

Then I will give them one heart and one way, that they may fear Me forever, for the good of them and their children after them   Jeremiah 32:39

A hardened heart is repulsive to God, His Word and His Will; it is not capable of receiving His blessing or favour.

Though Jesus had performed many miracles, but many of the Jews did not believe Him. And quoting from the prediction of Isaiah, an Old Testament Prophet, Jesus said:

He has blinded their eyes and hardened their hearts, lest they should see with their eyes, lest they should understand with their hearts and turn, so that I should heal them   John 12:40

A hardened heart needs to be "broken" and mellowed so that it can experience and reflect God's promise of "new things".

God, calling upon Judah to repentance, spoke through Jeremiah:

For thus said the LORD to the men of Judah and Jerusalem; break up your fallow ground, and sow not among thorns Jeremiah 4:3 KJV

Prophet Jeremiah told the people of Israel to "break up your fallow ground"; that is, to plough up the hardness of their hearts, just as a farmer ploughs up a fallow ground – soil that has not been tilled for a season.

God spoke through Prophet Hosea to confirm His message to His people: "break up your fallow ground (Hosea 10:12) or "plow up the hard ground of your hearts" (NLT). Nothing grows out of a stony ground.

Speaking on the parable of the sower, Jesus said: "Some fell on stony places, where they did not have much earth; and they immediately sprang up because they had no depth of earth... because they had no root, they withered away" (Matt. 13:5,6).

Explaining the parable of the sower, Jesus said:

But he who received the seed on the stony places, this is he who hears the word and immediately receives it with joy, yet he has no root in himself, but endures only for a while. For when tribulation or persecution arises because of the word, immediately he stumbles Matthew 13:20, 21

An evil heart breeds evil things, an "old heart" is a breeding ground for satanic activities; it is the source of evil.

Brood of vipers! How can you, being evil speak good things? For out of the abundance of the heart the mouth speaks. A good man out of the good treasure of his heart, brings forth good things, and an evil man out of the evil treasure brings forth evil things Matthew 12: 34, 35

Moreover, Satan uses careless, unregenerated hearts as his "workshop". As the "god of this world", Satan has blinded the hearts of evil men so that they may not positively respond to God's Word.

Whose minds the god of this age has blinded, who do not believe, lest the light of the gospel of the glory of Christ, who is the image of God, should shine on them 2 Cor. 4:4

Satan gained access to Judas' heart and prompted him to betray Jesus.

And supper being ended, the devil having now put into the heart of Judas Iscariot, Simon's son, to betray Him John 13:2 KJV

Satan also filled the heart of Ananias to lie to the Holy Spirit and deceive the church.

But Peter said, "Ananias, why has Satan filled your heart to lie to the Holy Spirit and keep back part of the price of the land for yourself? Acts 5:3

While Satan uses "old hearts" for evil purposes, God uses and blesses "new hearts" for His glory and for their benefits. He fills renewed hearts with His Spirit and new wisdom and willingness to accomplish new things and overcome new challenges.

God, speaking through Moses on artisan for building the tabernacle, said:

See, I have called by name Bezalel the son of Uri, the son of Hur, the tribe of Judah. And I have filled him with the Spirit of God, in wisdom, in understanding, in knowledge, and in all manner of workmanship. And I, indeed I, appointed with him Aholiab the son of Ahisamach, of the tribe of Dan; and I have put wisdom in the hearts of all the gifted artisans, that they may make all that I have commanded you Exodus 31:2, 3, 6.

The tabernacle offerings were presented by the artisans filled with renewed hearts and wisdom.

All the women who were gifted artisans spun yarn with their hands, and brought what they had spun, of blue, purple, and scarlet, and fine linen. All the women whose hearts stirred with wisdom spun yarn of goats' hair...And He has filled him with the spirit of God, in wisdom and understanding, in knowledge and all manner of workmanship Exodus 35: 25, 26, 31

Receiving A New heart

A new heart is not received by natural or scientific means; it is a Divine work; only God can change the heart, only God can give a new heart; only God can "circumcise" the heart.

God, speaking through Moses on the blessing of returning to Him (God), said:

And the Lord your God will circumcise your heart and the heart of your descendants, to love the Lord your God, with all your heart and with all your soul, that you may live Deuteronomy 30:6

This spiritual "surgery" is performed by the Holy Spirit- the Divine Agent for this change.

Paul writes:

But he is a Jew who is one inwardly; and circumcision is that of the heart, in the spirit, not in the letter, whose praise is not from men but from God. Romans 2:29

The Holy Spirit has been put within us to accomplish this transaction.

Speaking through Ezekiel on His promise of renewal for Israel God, said:

I will give you a new heart and put a new spirit within you; I will take the heart of stone out of your flesh and give you a heart of flesh Ezekiel 36:26

There are some Scriptural principles and pre-requisites for receiving a new heart. These include:

a.   Regeneration

Regeneration or New Birth qualifies us for a new heart; it is a Divine work wrought by the Holy Spirit within the Believer. According to Paul, the work of regeneration is "not by works of righteousness which we have done, but according to His mercy He saved us through the washing of regeneration and renewing of the Holy Spirit" (Tit. 3:5).

Another name for regeneration is "Born Again" (John 3:1-7).Only a regenerated soul can experience a new heart; this is what makes him or her a new creature, a new man or a brand new person.

Paul, writing on reconciliation to God, said:

Therefore, if anyone is in Christ, he is a new creation: old things have passed away, behold all things have become new
2 Corinthians 5:17

b.   Repentance

True repentance takes place in the heart; if we truly repent from the heart and genuinely turn to God, He will give us a new heart.

Writing to Israel on a call to repentance, Joel said:

"Now therefore", says the Lord' "turn to Me with all your heart, with fasting, with weeping and with mourning". So rend your heart, and not your garments, return to the Lord your God, for he is gracious and merciful, slow to anger, and of great kindness, and relents from doing harm.
Joel 2:12, 13

As a result of this heart – felt repentance, God has promised to restore His people and pour out His Spirit upon them.

We are told:

So I will restore to you the years that the swarming locust has eaten, the crawling locust, the consuming locust, and the chewing locust, My great army which I sent among you...And it shall come to pass afterward that I will pour out My Spirit on all flesh; your sons and your daughters shall prophesy, your old men will dream dreams, your young men shall see visions. And also on My menservants and on My maidservant I will pour My spirit in those days   Joel 2:25, 28, 29

c.   Prayer

When David was convicted of sin, he humbly acknowledged it and prayed – not only for Divine mercy, but also – for a new heart.

David prayed:

Have mercy upon me O God, according to your loving-kindness, according to the multitude of Your tender mercies, blot out my transgressions, wash me thoroughly from my iniquity, and cleanse me from my sin.   For   I   acknowledge   my transgressions, and my sin is always before me Psalm 51:1-3

But in verse 10, David said:

Create in me a clean heart, O God, and renew a steadfast Spirit within me

Like David, we should pray that God should create a clean heart in us and renew a right spirit within us.

Paul reminds Christians that self discipline is what can help us. Therefore he urged Christians to guard their attitudes and to replace worry with prayer and think on the positive things that edify. The peace of God will guard our hearts and minds, keeping them focused on Christ.

Be careful for nothing; but in everything by prayer and supplication with thanksgiving let your requests be made known unto God. And the peace of God, which passeth all understanding, shall keep your hearts and minds through Christ Jesus Phil 4: 6, 7 (KJV)

d.   Waiting Upon The Lord

Spiritual renewal comes by waiting upon the Lord. As we patiently wait upon God, He will renew our inner man. And with this inward renewal comes renewed strength, renewed zeal and renewed power for exploits.

God is a wise Counselor and Provider who is the source for every need we may have, as epitomised by Isaiah in Isaiah 40:31:

But those who wait on the Lord shall renew their strength; they shall mount up with wings like eagles, they shall run and not be weary, they shall walk and not faint Isaiah 40:31

e.   Consecration

Consecration means to set apart oneself from sin unto God; it means to hallow, to make sacred, holy, sanctify or to dedicate oneself for the service of God.   Consecration helps us to surrender totally to the will of God and yield ourselves totally for His use and glory.

Writing on the need to present ourselves to God as living sacrifices as Christians, Paul said:

I beseech you therefore, brethren, by the mercies of God, that you present your bodies a living sacrifice, holy; acceptable to God which is your reasonable service. And do not be conform to this world, but be transformed by the renewing of your mind, that you may prove what is that good and acceptable and perfect will of God   Romans 12: 1-2

In the process of consecration we experience spiritual renewal in the totality of our being – both inwardly, spirit, soul, mind and heart – and outwardly, that is, the body (see 1 Thes 5:23).

Peter also wrote:

But sanctify the Lord in your hearts, and be ready always to give a defence to anyone who asks a reason for the hope that is in you, with meekness and fear 1 Peter 3:15

f.   Faith

Faith is defined as "the substance of things hoped for, the evidence of things not seen" (Heb 11:1 KJV) or "the confidence that what we hope for will actually happen; it gives us assurance about things we cannot see" (NLT). Faith is the channel by which we receive redemptive blessings; through faith we receive salvation, healing, blessings, sanctification and gifts of the Spirit. When we pray, we should believe that what we ask for will be answered. We can believe God to change our heart and mind when we pray.

We are taught by Jesus:

Therefore I say to you, whatever things you ask when you pray, believe that you

receive them, and you will have them
Mark 11:24

The heart is purified and renewed in response to faith.

Luke wrote:

So God, who knows the heart, acknowledge them by giving them the Holy Spirit, just as He did to us and made no distinction between us and them, purifying their hearts by faith Acts 15:8 , 9

g. The Word of God

The Word of God has sanctifying and cleansing power; it can purify the heart and make it new.

The Psalmist writes:

How can a young man cleanse his way? By taking heed according to Your Word.
Psalm 119:9

We are told:

You are already clean because of the word which I have spoken to you John 15:3

Sanctify them by Your truth, Your word is truth John 17:17

To experience this purifying power of the Word, we should saturate our hearts with the Word of God.

Writing on the character of the new man, Paul counseled:

Let the word of Christ dwell in you richly in all wisdom, teaching and admonishing one another in Psalms and hymns and spiritual songs, singing with grace in our heart to the Lord Colossians 3:16

God commanded the children of Israel to keep His word in their heart:

And these words which I command you today shall be in your heart. Deuteronomy 6:6

As you keep the Lord's word in your heart, may you be sanitised, blessed, lifted and receive new strength to do great exploits.

Chapter 11

RENEWED FOR NEW THINGS

The renewal of the totality of man – body, soul and spirit – is necessary for a healthy, successful and productive life. We are kept refreshed and receive new strength to face new challenges, do new things and soar higher to new heights in life and ministry. Moreover, we can live longer and be more useful in this life, when we are constantly being renewed.

Every car needs to be regularly serviced; the oil needs to be changed and every faulty part needs to be repaired or replaced, where necessary. Thus, the car can run faster and smoother and last longer.

As humans, we too, need this regular "servicing" and "repair". We are liable to become weak and tired as we grow older. Even in spiritual realms, we have "infirmities" (Rom 8:26-27) and therefore, need to be regularly renewed by the Holy Spirit.

The strongest among us can become tired, discouraged, weary and faint- sometimes. But God can give power to the faint and increase the strength of weak saints.

Isaiah writes:

He gives power to the weak and to those who have no might He increase strength. Even the youth shall faint and be weary, and the young men shall utterly fall Isaiah 40:29, 30

What Is Renewal?

To "renew" means to restore strength or vigour – physically, mentally, emotionally and spiritually. It means to restore to a new or fresh condition; to replace an old or worn-out part with a new part. It is synonymous with renovate, rebuild, revive, revitalize, refresh, repair or re-energize.

In the Old Testament the two words used for "renew" are chadash and chalaph. The former, chadash, means to be new, to rebuild, to repair – that is, to put right, overhaul or make fit for use again. It is the word used by David, when he prayed for forgiveness.

Create in me a clean heart O, God, and renew a right spirit within me Psalm 51:10 (KJV)

When David prayed for God to "renew a right spirit within" him, he was simply asking God to "overhaul" or "revive" his old sinful heart – so that his inward thoughts and desires might be right in God's sight. David, who had been "a man after God's heart" (1 Sam 13:14), seemed to have lost the purity and freshness of his heart. He had allowed lustful thoughts and evil desires to fill his heart, which led to his adulterous relationship with Bathsheba – the wife of Uriah, one of his loyal soldiers, whom he also killed to cover up his sin (2 Sam.11: 1-16).

In Psalm 51, David humbly acknowledged his sin and asked for forgiveness. He was truly remorseful for his adultery with Bathsheba and for killing her husband.

In his confession, David reveals some profound theological truths about human nature and sin, and the need for inward renewal by the Spirit of God.

First, we are all born sinners.

Behold, I was brought forth in iniquity, and in sin my mother conceived me
Psalm 51:5

This scripture speaks about the origin of sin, and its universality. Sin is a universal inheritance, resulting from the Fall: "For all have sinned, and come short of the glory of God" (Rom 3: 23); "who can say, I have made my heart clean, I am pure from my sin" (Prov. 20:9); "If we say we have no sin, we deceive ourselves, and the truth is not in us" (1 John 1:8; See also: 1 King 8:46; Isa 53: 6; 64:6 etc).

Secondly, the heart-as the center of life- is the source of sin.

Jesus said:

But those things which proceed out of the mouth come from the heart, and they defile a man. For out of the heart proceed evil thoughts, murders, adulteries, fornications, thefts, false witness, blasphemies. Mathew 15:18, 19

We were born sinners, from the moment we were conceived in our mother's wombs. Because we are born sinners, our natural inclination is to please ourselves and satisfy our lustful desires – rather than God. This was what happened to David when he took Uriah's wife. However, David acknowledged the need to be inwardly cleansed and purified from his natural inclinations.

Have mercy upon me, O God, according to Your loving kindness, according to the multitude of Your tender mercies, blot out my transgressions... Purge me with hyssop, and I shall be clean, wash me and I shall be whiter than snow. Psalm 51:2,7

Like David, we should recognize our natural inclinations and weaknesses and ask God for inward cleansing and renewing of our heart, by His Spirit.

This renewal will fill our hearts and spirit with new and pure thoughts and desires. From this renewed heart and spirit, proceeds right desires, right thoughts and right behaviour.

The same Hebrew word is used by David, in Psalm 103:5; he said:

Who satisfies your mouth with good things, so that your youth is renewed like the eagles Psalm 103:5

David speaks of his youth being "renewed" like the eagles. This "renewal", is a constant experience and is one of the redemptive benefits mentioned in verses 1-5, including forgiveness, healing and Divine protection.

Bless the Lord, O my soul; and all that is within me, bless, His holy name! Bless the Lord O my soul, and forget not all His benefits. Who forgives all your iniquities, who heals all your diseases; who redeems your life from destruction, and who crowns you with loving-kindness and tender mercies, who satisfies your mouth with good things, so that your youth is renewed like the eagles Psalm 103: 1-5

This "renewal" of youth is compared to that of the eagles. David's experience harmonies with Isaiah's admonition. According to Prophet Isaiah, we are constantly renewed, as we wait upon the Lord; thus we can soar high with wings like the eagles.

But those who wait on the Lord shall renew their strength; they shall mount up with wings like eagles, they shall run and not be weary, they shall walk and not faint Isaiah 40:31

Isaiah used the second Hebrew word chalaph for "renew", which denotes to change, to spring up, to sprout, or renew. It is also used in Isa. 41:1; "and let the people renew their strength". But it is used in Isa. 40:31, in the same sense as, Psalm 103:5, that is, renewal like the eagles.

Why like the eagle's?

The eagle is used in both scriptures as a metaphor for spiritual renewal and soaring to new heights. The eagle is the highest soaring bird; it is naturally endowed with soaring power which makes it soar higher than other birds. Eagles naturally "renew their strength" after soaring. They do this by growing new feathers, which constitute their wings.

The secret of the eagle's soaring power lies in its wings. They have strong and healthy feathers which make their wings strong; these feathers enhance their natural ability to glide through the wind and soar to great heights - far beyond the limits of other birds.

From time to time, after soaring, the eagle stays on the mountain, where it changes its old, weak feathers to grow new ones; and with new feathers come new strength in old age. This is a type of "waiting". During this period, the old eagle's strength is renewed like that of a young eagle, so that it is ready and fit to soar again – even to new and higher heights.

This was what David experienced when he testified:

He fills my life with good things! My youth is renewed like the eagle's! Psalm 103:5; Living Bible

It is this periodic changing of the eagle's feathers that keeps the old eagle youthful, soaring with "renewed strength", vigour and agility, as though it were a young eagle. Thus, the old eagle is never too old, never tired to soar and never retiring.

The "renewing of strength" is borrowed from the growing of fresh feathers by eagles. Thus, to "renew their strength" implies to put on new strength as eagles grow new feathers. To grow "new feathers", we need to "put off old feathers" – we must put away the "old man" and put on the "new man".

There are some old things we need to give up, to gain new strength.

Paul emphasized in Hebrew 12 that the Christian race must be run with passion, patience, purpose and perspective.

Therefore we also, since we are surrounded by so great a cloud of witnesses, let us lay aside every weight, and the sin which so easily ensnares us, and let us run with endurance the race that is set before us Hebrews 12:1

We are told:

The night is far spent, the day is at hand. Therefore let us cast off the works of darkness, and let us put on the armour of light Romans 13:12

Paul also reminded the Ephesians' church "to be renewed in the spirit of your mind" (Ephes. 4:23).

Our strength needs to be renewed to meet the challenges of aging. God can renew our strength – physically, emotionally, mentally and spiritually. He has made abundant provisions for us, through His Word. Thus, even in old age, we never "retire", but are "refired" to do new exploits in ministry and warfare.

The righteous shall flourish like a palm tree, and shall grow like a cedar in

Lebanon. Those who are planted in the house of the lord shall flourish in the courts of our God. They shall still bear fruit in old age; they shall be fresh and flourishing Psalm 92:12 -14

As you wait upon the Lord – through prayer, reading and meditating on the Word – you will "grow new feathers as the eagle's". This way, you will "run and not be weary; and ... walk and not faint" (Isa. 40:31).

You will never be irrelevant or useless or forced to retire prematurely; but you will wax stronger and stronger, and be fit to soar to new heights, attempt new things and accomplish new things for God and His church.

This was the experience of Caleb – the "old soldier" who was never too old to take the mountain. At the age of 85 years, Caleb felt as strong as he was at 40 years. He felt he was strong enough to do more exploits, take the mountain, drive out the giants and possess his possession.

I was forty years old when Moses the servant of the Lord sent me from Kadesh Barnea to spy out the land, and I brought back word to him as was in my heart. ...And now behold, the Lord has kept me alive, as He said, these forty – five years, ever since the Lord spoke this word to Moses, while Israel wandered in the wilderness, and now, here I am this day eighty-five years old. As yet I am as strong this day as on the day that Moses sent me just as my strength was then, so now is my strength for war, both for going out and for coming in. Now therefore, give me this mountain of which the Lord spoke in that day; for which you heard in that day how the Anakim were there, and that the cities were great and fortified. It may be that the Lord will be with me, and I shall be able to drive them out as the Lord said. Joshua 14: 7, 10-12

Let us take note of verse 11

As yet I am as strong this day as on the day that Moses sent me; just as my strength was then, so now is my strength for war, both for going out and for coming in.

In the New Testament, Paul used two Greek words for "renewal". The first is the Greek verb anakainoo, which means to renew, to make new. It is made up of ana (back or again) and kainos ("new" – not recent, but different). It is the word used by Paul, of the daily renewal of "the inward man". He said:

Therefore we do not lose heart. Even though our outward man is perishing, yet the inward man is being renewed day by day 2 Corinthians 4:16

The word is used here for "renewal" of spiritual strength – "the inward man" – in contrast to the physical form or physical body. Paul also uses the word in Col. 3:10, of the "new man", in contrast to the old, unregenerate nature.

We are told to put off the old, like taking off a worn-out set of clothes, so as to put on the new (Colo. 3:8 -11).

And have put on the new man who is renewed in knowledge according to the image of him who created him Colossians 3:10

According to Paul, "the new man is renewed in knowledge" (KJV). In the Living Bible, it reads: "You are living a brand new kind of life that is continually learning more and more of what is right, and trying constantly to be more like Christ who created this new life within you". And, in the New Living Translation, it reads: "Put on your new nature, and be renewed as you learn to know your Creator and become like Him".

As we can see, from the various translations, the text teaches two facts about "renewal". First, this renewing is attained through spiritual knowledge of God and His Word. The more we know Him – intimately through prayer and through His Word – the more we become spiritually renewed. This renewing is a "learning process" – we are continually learning more and more.

We are told:

Then Jesus said to those Jews who believed Him; "If you abide by My word, you are My disciples indeed. And you shall know the truth, and the truth shall make you free" John 8: 31, 32

Apostle Peter gave this admonition:

Therefore, laying aside all malice, all deceit, hypocrisy, envy, and all evil speaking as new born babes, desire the pure milk of the word that you may grow thereby. 1 Peter 2:1-2

Writing on fruitful growth in faith Peter said:

But also for this very reason, giving all diligence, add to your faith, virtue, to virtue knowledge, to knowledge self-control, to self control perseverance, to perseverance godliness, to godliness brotherly kindness, and to brotherly kindness love. For if these things are yours and abound, you will be neither barren nor unfruitful in the knowledge of our Lord Jesus Christ. 2 Peter 1: 5- 8

We are told:

But grow in the grace and knowledge of our Lord and Saviour Jesus Christ. To Him be the glory both now and forever   2 Peter 3:18

Secondly, we grow to become Christ-like, as the "new man" is constantly being renewed. The more we know Him, and the closer we walk with Him, the more we will become like Him. Thus, we increasingly become God-like or Christ-like in our thoughts, and desires, which reflect in our character or conduct.

This was perhaps what Paul meant when he said:

That I may know Him and the power of His resurrection, and the fellowship of His sufferings, being conformed to His death Philippians 3:10

Again, he said:

Who will transform our lowly body that it may be conformed to His glorious body, according to the working by which He is able even to subdue all things to Himself Philippians 3:21

Peter said:

By which have been given to us exceedingly great and precious promises, that through these you may be partakers of divine nature, having escaped the corruption that is in the word through lust 2 Peter 1:4

The noun form of the Greek verb is anakainosis, which means a renovation, "a renewal", it is used for "renewing" in Rom 12:2 and Tit. 3:5.

In Rom. 12:2, Paul said:

And be not conformed to this world: but be ye transformed by the renewing of your mind... Rom 12:2 (KJV)

Through consistent consecration, holy living (Rom 12:1) and non- conforming to the values of this world, God transforms us into a new person, changing the way we think and live to conform to His own standard. This inward transformation is produced by the Holy Spirit; for we are saved "by the washing of regeneration and renewing of the Holy Ghost" (Tit 3:5 KJV). The Holy Spirit controls our hearts and re-educates and redirects our minds and feelings, from carnal mindedness to spiritual mindedness. Thus, we can truly please God and experience a joyful life and peace.

Paul said:

That the righteous requirement of the law might be fulfilled in us who do not walk according to the flesh but according to the spirit. For those who live according to the flesh set their minds on the things of the flesh, but those who live according to the Spirit, the things of the Spirit. For to be carnally minded is death, but to be spiritually minded is life and peace.
Romans 8: 4-6

Paul also used another related Greek word for "renewal"; he urged the Ephesians Christians to "be renewed in the spirit of your mind", in the same way as Paul urged the Romans in Rom 12:2.

That you put off, concerning your former conduct, the old man which grows corrupt according to the deceitful lusts, and be renewed in the spirit of your mind, and that you put on the new man which was created according to God, in true righteousness and holiness Ephesians 4:22-24

In verse 23, Paul said, "be renewed in the spirit of your mind" or "let the Spirit renew your thoughts and attitude" " (NLT) or "your attitude must be constantly changing for the better" (LB).

The Greek word used in verse 23 is ananeoo, which denotes to make new, make young, to renovate, reform, renew.

According to W. E. Vine:

The renewal here mentioned is not that of the mind itself in its natural powers of memory, judgment, and perception, but"the spirit of the mind", which, under the controlling power of the indwelling Holy Spirit, directs its bent and energies Godward in the enjoyment of "fellowship with the Father and with His Son, Jesus Christ", and of the fulfillment of the will of God. 9

....
9. W. E. Vine, Vine's Concise Dictionary of Bible Words, Nashville, Tennessee: Thomas Nelson Inc., 1999, P. 310.

Chapter 12

RENEWED FOR NEW EXPLOITS: EXAMPLES

As it was discussed in chapter 11, all humans are liable to be weak, feel tired, or grow weary. Only God never grows weak, tired or weary. He is the same today as He was in eternity past, and He will be the same throughout future eternity (Heb. 13:8). Therefore, He can give power to the weak and strength to the powerless.

God the wise Counselor and Provider, asserts His Authority and Power as the Source of everything when He spoke through Prophet Isaiah:

Have you not known? Have you not heard? The everlasting God, the Lord, the creator of the ends of the earth never faints nor is weary. His understanding is unsearchable. He gives power to the weak, and to those who have no might He increase strength Isaiah 40:28, 29

In this life – as long as we live in this mortal, unresurrected body – we will go through the normal challenges of life. And, as we age, our strength diminishes. We were not created to live permanently in this world; our present bodies make us groan, and this trend will continue until when we are resurrected. Then our bodies will be changed (1 Cor. 15:51-52);

we will have new bodies that will be adaptable to the conditions of life in eternity – where we will never grow old.

Paul, writing on assurance of the resurrection, said:

For we know that if our earthly house, this tent, is destroyed, we have a building from God, a house not made with hands, eternal in the heavens. For in this we groan, earnestly desiring to be clothed with our habitation which is from heaven, if indeed, having been clothed we shall not be found naked. For we who are in this tent groan, being burdened, not because we want to be unclothed, but further clothed, that mortality may be swallowed up by life 2 Corinthians 5: 1-4

Life in this world is imperfect. All creatures – including us, who are saved and have the Holy Spirit within us – feel the pains and limitations of this imperfection. Paul wrote about this in his epistle to the Christians in Rome.

Because the creation itself also will be delivered from the bondage of corruption into the glorious liberty of the children of God. For we know that the whole creation groans and labours with birth pangs together until now. Not only that, but we also who have the first fruits of the Spirit, even ourselves groan within ourselves;

eagerly waiting for the adoption, the redemption of our body Romans 8:21-23

Unlike the unsaved, however, the Holy Spirit within us helps us to overcome the challenges of our "infirmities" or frailties. The Holy Spirit helps us to have victory over our daily challenges and in our praying. The Holy Spirit helps us daily to continue in God's service, without feeling weak.

Paul reminds Christians how the Holy Spirit navigates life for us.

Likewise the Spirit helps in our weaknesses. For we do not know what we should pray for as we ought, but the Spirit Himself makes intercession for us with groaning which cannot be uttered. Now He who searches the hearts knows what the mind of the Spirit is, because He makes intercession for the saints according to the will of God Romans 8:26, 27

The Holy Spirit helps us to do things we could not do by our own power; He strengthens the "inner man" so that we do not break down, or give up. And while the outward man may gradually diminish, the inward man is being renewed every day.

According to Paul, the inner man in believers is growing every day, though our physical bodies may be dying.

Therefore we do not lose heart. Even though our outward man is perishing, yet the inward man is being renewed day by day 2 Corinthians 4:16

This chapter is a continuation from the previous chapter on "Renewed For New Things". My focus here will be on examples of "renewed" people who accomplished new exploits.

In these examples, we learn how God's anointed men became tired, discouraged and almost gave up. But after being divinely renewed, they received spiritual strength to continue in ministry, with new breakthroughs and doing new exploits.

Prophet Jonah

a.   Who Was Jonah?

Jonah, son of Amittai, called as a prophet, a contemporary of Jeroboam II of Israel (2 Kings 14:25), from Gath Hepher, three miles north of Nazareth, so Jonah was a Galilean.

Divine call came to Jonah; "Arise, go to Nineveh, (capital city of Assyria) that great city, and cry out against it for their wickedness has come before Me". (Jonah 1:2). God is concerned for the Gentiles as well as for His covenant people Israel. But God's prophet and messenger did not want to proclaim the message for fear that the Assyrians would respond and be spared by the compassionate God. Jonah's reluctance did not take the form of verbal argument, he simply ran in the opposite direction – Tarshish (to the west) as against northeast to Nineveh.

But soon Jonah discovered that called leaders cannot run from God. The Psalmist asked: "Where can I go from your spirit? Or where can I flee from Your presence?" (Psalm 139:7) Jonah's sin found him out inside the ship where some frightened sailors threw him overboard and a huge fish (whale) swallowed the run-away prophet. Over the next three days Jonah had become sober, he realized that it was a fearful thing to fall into the hand of God. (Jonah 1: 1-17)

b.   The Effect of Divine Chastisement

(a)   Jonah's prayer and repentance in the fish's belly (Jonah 2: 1-6).

Jonah prayed fervently in the belly of the fish; he cried out that God should deliver him from his afflictions. "For You have cast me into the deep, into the heart of the seas, and the flood surrounded me; all Your billows and your waves passed over me." Then I said, "I have been cast out of Your sight; yet I will look again toward Your holy temple" (Jonah 2:3,4).

God will always chastise and discipline His erring children; but He will never forsake them. "For whom the Lord loves He chastens, and scourges every son He receives" (Heb. 12:6).

One can only imagine the wretched conditions inside the animal God had prepared to temporarily house Jonah. But was it any worse than the situations into which we put ourselves when we run from God? Eventually the Lord will bring us to a place where we have little choice but to stop, listen and obey. But why wait for such an unpleasant place?

(b) Jonah had a new experience and vowed to start afresh

The three days experience in the belly of the fish became a reminder to Jonah of the sovereignty of God in every circumstance. In his unique "prayer closet", Jonah uttered declarative praise psalm and remembered the Lord and prayed passionately to Him.

When my soul fainted within me, I remembered the Lord, and my prayer went to You, into your holy temple. Those who regard worthless idols forsake their own mercy Jonah 2:7, 8

Jonah offered thanksgiving for his deliverance from drowning. When he acknowledged that "salvation is of the Lord" (Jonah 2:9), he was finally willing to obey and be used by God.

c.   Jonah Renewed to Serve Again

Jonah was restored and given a second chance to serve again. After he was cast up on the shore, Jonah had a long time to reflect on his experiences during his eastward trek of hundreds of mile to Nineveh.

(a)   God answered Jonah's prayer

So the Lord spoke to the fish, and it vomited Jonah unto dry land   Jonah 2:10

Consequently, Jonah obeyed his second commission to go to Nineveh (Jonah 3: 1-4), where he became "a sign to the Ninevites" (Luke 11:30).

(b)   Jonah's renewed mission

God recommissioned Jonah to go to Nineveh and preach the earlier message given to him in (Jonah 1: 1-2). Thus, the runaway prophet listened with rapt attention, ready to proceed on his assignment.

(c) Jonah's new zeal for his new mission

Jonah was recommissioned, empowered and re-energised for the new assignment. The disobedient prophet chose to run with God following the Lord's offer of a second chance. "So Jonah arose and went to Nineveh, according to the word of the Lord." (Jonah 3:3). When God speaks, man must obey. Obedience is not only highly rewarding, but it produces the best result.

He made a journey that would have lasted for three days in one day. It was a distance of seventy-two (72) miles, but his renewed attitude gave him the strength to make the journey within a short time; his renewed life gave him fresh zeal, fresh spirit and fresh vision for his new mission.

(d) The result of Jonah's mission in Nineveh

As Jonah proceeded through the city, his one-sentence sermon brought incredible results. It was the most responsible evangelistic effort in history. Jonah's message of coming judgment was followed by a proclamation by the king of the city to fast and repent (Jonah 3:4-9). God in His great mercy "relented from the disaster that He said that He would bring upon the people of Nineveh" (Jonah 3:10).

What can we learn from Jonah's story?

Despite Jonah's disobedience, lack of focus, cultural prejudice, wrong motives, and self-righteousness, God never gave up on him. Sometimes God uses us in spite of our shortcomings and inadequacies. Many reluctant leaders have been used to accomplish His gracious mission and uncommon exploits.

Leaders should always remember that He who calls us to the ministry is faithful. Therefore, we should do God's work in God's way; He will surely reward our faithfulness by blessing us and increasing the seed, we sow (1 Cor. 3:6, 7; 4:2).

Samson

a.   Who Was Samson?

Samson was a son of Manoah, a Danite who judged Israel for twenty years. He was one of the most outstanding of the Hebrew judges. He was unique in the way his birth and manner of life were foretold. The angel of God appeared to Mrs. Manoah and said to her; "Indeed now, you are barren and have borne no children, but you shall conceive and bear a son. Now therefore, please be careful not to drink wine or similar drink, and not to eat anything unclean. For behold, you shall conceive and bear a son. And no razor shall come upon his head, for the child shall be a Nazirite to God from the womb; and he shall begin to deliver Israel out of the hand of the Philistines" (Judges 13:3-7).

The woman conceived according to the message of the angel and the child was named Samson and "the child grew and God blessed him". Consequently, the Lord anointed him and he started his ministry in earnest.

And the Spirit of Lord began to move upon him at Mahaneh Dan between Zorah and Eshtoal Judges 13:25

b.　His Exploits

As long as Samson remained a Nazirite, he was unconquerable.　Unlike other judges who networked with others to accomplish their assignments, Samson did everything single handedly and alone. Samson never called the armies of Israel together; he asked for no assistance. What he did, he did alone in his own unconquerable strength.

When a young lion came rearing against him:

And the spirit of the Lord came mightily upon him, and he tore the lion apart as one would have torn apart a young goat, though he had nothing in his hand... Judges 14:6

Samson killed one thousand (1,000) Philistines with a fresh jawbone of a donkey.

With the jawbone of a donkey, heaps upon heaps, with the jawbone of a donkey I have slain a thousand men Judges 15:16

He carried the gate of Gaza, "with the two gate posts, right out of the ground. He put them on his shoulders and carried them to the top of the mountain across from Hebron!" (Judges 16:3 LB).

c.   Samson lost his glory and power

The complex story of Samson teaches us the evils of mixed or foreign marriages (Judg. 14:3), the laxity of sexual relations and playing with temptation. (Judg. 16:1-21).

The deadly results of Samson's self-indulgence after he broke his Nazirite vow, appear in their dark and ominous order:

*   Self - confidence: "I will go out as before"(Judges 16:20).
*   Self – ignorance: "He did not know that the Lord had departed from him" (Judg. 16:21)
*   Self – weakness: "The Philistines laid hold on him" (Judg. 16:21)
*   Self – darkness: "They put out his eyes" (Jug. 16:21)
*   Self – degradation: "They brought him down to Gaza" (Judg. 16: 1-3, 21).

*   Self – bondage: "They bound him with fetters" (Judg. 16:21)
*   Self – drudgery: "He did grind in the prison house" (Judg. 16:21).
*   Self – humiliation: "Call for Samson that he may make us sport" (Judg. 16:25).

In spite of his self-destruction God did not abandon Samson.

d.   Samson's Renewal: His hair began to grow again

Samson learned the hard way that trust and holiness provides the foundation for all genuine and successful leadership. "However, the hair of his head began to grow again after it had been shaven" Judg. 16:22).

Moreover, Samson received a new spirit and fresh passion for ministry. He prayed earnestly for a second chance.

Then Samson called to the Lord, saying, "O Lord God remember me, I pray! Strengthen me, I pray, just this once, O God, that I may with one blow take vengeance on the Philistines for my two eyes!" Judges 16:28

Let us note the following acts that brought renewal to Samson:
-      Samson called upon the Lord – he remembered God, the sources of his strength.

- Samson repented genuinely.
- He prayed earnestly for spiritual strength
- He prayed to be remembered – "this once" – one more time

e.   Samson's New Exploit After Renewal

Then Samson said; "Let me die with the Philistines!" And he pushed with all his might, and the temple fell on the lords and all the people who were in it. So the dead that he killed at his death were more than he had killed in his life Judges 16:30

According to verse 27, Samson slew the five Philistine leaders who were there as well as 3,000 people in the balconies who were watching him and making fun of him. Thus, he was better in the end than at the beginning of his ministry.

f.   What lesson can we learn from Samson's life?

Great lessons of spiritual and moral values can be learnt-especially his restoration, new zeal and exploit after his fall.

Samson stands out as a man of striking contrasts. He had a noble beginning and was separated as a Nazirite (Judg. 13:5), mighty in physical strength (Judg. 16:3, 9,13, 14), yet weak in resisting temptation (Judg. 16:15-17).

From the life of Samson, leaders should address their glaring character, weaknesses and learn not to misuse their God–given gifts or toy with God's anointing.

Leaders should learn that the fall of a man is not the end of his life. They should always keep hope alive. God will not forsake His people forever. Micah wrote: "Do not rejoice over me, my enemy; when I fall, I will arise; when I sit in darkness, the Lord will be a light to me" (Micah 7:8).

God became a light again to Samson when his hair started to grow. He was given a second chance; he was alive with new hope, new opportunity, new confidence, new strength and a new zeal for new exploit, after his fall.

Whatever may be your setback or the negative situation you are passing through, God has not forsaken you. Remember: when there is life, there is hope. Our Lord is conciliatory, call upon Him and repent from your sin; you will encounter His mercy (Prov. 28:13). God is always ready to receive back His misguided children.

The Psalmist wrote:

The steps of a good man are ordered by the Lord, and He delights in his way. Though he falls, he shall not be utterly

cast down; for the Lord upholds him with His hand   Psalm 37:23, 24

This is your new day – a new dawn. Rise up and accept the second chance offered by God through His Son, Jesus Christ, who is always ready to forgive. God is ready to arm you with His offensive and defensive weapon to do new exploits. You will serve God with new zeal, fresh anointing and new vision. Your latter end shall surely be greater than the former and you will be glad you accepted the second chance.

Elijah The Tishbite

a.   Who was Elijah?

Elijah, the Tishbite, was of the inhabitants of Gilead (1 Kings 17:1). The bible paints the picture of this great prophet as an iron man, fearless, bold and a dauntless reformer (1 Kgs. 18:17 -46). He was a rebuke of kings (1 Kgs. 21:20; 2 Kgs 1:16). Elijah lived during the reigns of Ahab and Ahaziah in the northern kingdom of Israel. He was called to denounce the idolatry of Israel and the wickedness of Ahab and to pronounce God's judgment (1 Kgs 16:30-33). Elijah was called during a very sad time in the history of Israel, when the people had all turned their backs on God and their king had sinned against God openly and boldly.

b.   Elijah's Exploits on Mount Carmel

Elijah, consumed with holy indignation, prayed that it might not rain in Israel – and for more than three years, not a drop of rain fell. Later, all alone, the prophet on Mount Carmel among 450 prophets of Baal, gave the people the visual proof of the impotence of their puny god.

(a) The challenge

Elijah challenged Baal worshippers and his prophets:

"How long will you falter between two opinions? If the Lord is God, follow Him; but if Baal, follow him ..." Elijah said to the people, "I alone am left a prophet of the Lord; but Baal's prophets are four hundred and fifty men. Therefore let them give us two bulls; and let them choose one bull for themselves, cut it in pieces and lay it on the wood, but put no fire under it; and I will prepare the other bull and lay it on the wood, but put no fire under it. Then you will call on the name of your gods, and I will call on the name of the Lord, and the God who answers by fire, He is God. So the people answered and said; it is well spoken!!" 1 Kings 18:21-24

(b)   The Fire

The prophets of Baal did everything including cutting themselves with knives but there was no fire. Later in the evening, Elijah prepared the altar, cut the bull, dug trenches around the altar and urged the people to pour water on the sacrifice. He prayed a short prayer and God sent fire to consume the sacrifice (1 Kings 18: 36-38).There was a spontaneous reaction from the people when they saw the sacrifice consumed by fire. "The Lord He is God! The Lord, He is God" (Kings 18:39).

(c)   The Rain

To bring the drought to an end, Elijah prayed for rain; "Then Elijah said to Ahab, "go up, eat and drink; for there is the sound of abundance of rain" (1 Kings 18:41). It was a sweet end of a dramatic proof of God's supremacy over Baal and a misguided people. God sent the rain to put an end to over three years drought in the land.

(d)   The Prophets of Baal and grove slain

Prophet Elijah did not allow the false prophets who had misled the people for a very long time to escape without paying with their lives for deceiving the people of God to serve strange gods. At the instance of Elijah, the people grabbed the 850 prophets of Baal and grove and they were all executed.

c.   Jezebel's Threat

Notwithstanding his great exploits on Mount Carmel, Elijah was threatened.

And Ahab told Jezebel all that Elijah had done, and also how he had executed all the prophets with the sword. Then Jezebel sent a message to Elijah saying; so let the gods do to me, and more also if I do not make your life as the life of one of them by tomorrow about this time 1 Kings 19: 1, 2

Jezebel's threat had a profound negative effect on Elijah; he was afraid and fled for his life.

Elijah escaped from Jezebel by undertaking a day's journey (twenty four miles) into the wilderness (1 Kgs 19:3-5). This action portrays Elijah as a man prone to discouragement (1 Kgs 19:4 9-14) and a man capable of fallible judgment (1 Kings 19: 4, 18).

d.   Elijah's Renewal and Restoration

In spite of Elijah's discouragement, God did not abandon him, he sent an angel to provide him with bread and water. "Thus as he lay and slept under a broom tree, suddenly an angel touched him. And said to him, arise and eat" (1 Kings 19:5).

Elijah was divinely touched; he had a second touch from the Lord which was an offer of a second chance. A second touch is an assurance that one has not been forsaken, an approval or assurance of God's presence. This second touch provided the encouragement he needed; he was divinely encouraged.

And the angel of the lord came back the second time and touched him and said; arise and eat, because the journey is too great for you 1 Kings 19:7

God is the best partner you can have; in times of low morale, disappointment or frustration, He offers His right hand of fellowship and encouragement.

e.   Elijah's New Strength and New Zeal

Following this Divine visitation and new touch, Elijah received new strength, fresh anointing and fresh passion to continue his ministry.

We are told:

So he arose, and ate and drank; and he went in the strength of that food forty days and forty nights as far as Horeb, the mountain of God   1 Kings 19:8

f.   Elijah's New Assignments

In the wilderness, the overwrought prophet suffered a lapse of confidence but he was quickly restored and given new assignments; to anoint Hazael as king over Syria; to anoint Jehu, as king over Israel; and to anoint Elisha as his successor (1 Kings 19: 15-21).

g. Elijah's Fresh Authority and Power

When Ahaziah, the king of Israel injured himself in a fall, he wanted to know whether he would recover but he inquired of the false god, Baal, not the God of Israel. This angered the Lord who sent a prophecy through Elijah to the king informing him that he would die. The king in turn sent a captain and fifty soldiers to arrest Elijah, but the prophet called down fire from heaven and killed them. After this happened a second time to another group of soldiers, a third delegation approached Elijah and begged for mercy. An angel told Prophet Elijah to go with the men to visit the king (2 Kings 1:1-17). Thus, Elijah demonstrated the full proof of divine call on his life and God proved Himself strong on his behalf despite Elijah's shortcomings. One with God is truly a majority.

What lessons can we learn from Elijah's life and exploits – before and after his renewal?

Even great men can be discouraged and tempted to give up. But God can renew, refire and recommission his weak servants. He gave

Elijah bread (the word – spiritual food) and water (the Holy Spirit) – which gave him strength for 40 days journey.

Prophet Jeremiah

a.   Jeremiah's Early Life and Calling

God called Jeremiah, the son of Hilkiah, as a prophet from Anathoth in the land of Benjamin in the days of Josiah, the son of Amon the last good king from Judah (Jer. 1:1-3). The man was born a priest from the line of Abiathar (2 Chr. 35: 25; 36:12) but became a prophet by divine call. The prophet's leadership came at a time of moral, political, and religious decline, ending in the Babylonian exile. God called Jeremiah as a youth and immediately began to prepare him to serve as a prophet to the nations. He was a priest called to prophetic service at a most unhappy time. Without doubt, prophet Jeremiah recorded one of the toughest assignments of any leader in the Old Testament. God called him to lead a stubborn people, then informed him that the people would not follow his lead (Jer. 7:27, 28).

The circumstances of God's call on Jeremiah's life are outlined in Jer. 1:4-10 as follows:

· God created Jeremiah for a purpose (verse 5)
· Jeremiah felt inadequate (verse6)
· God wanted total control (verse 7).

161

· God gave a promise of a blessing (verse 8).
· God gave Jeremiah spiritual anointing (verse 9).
· God gave Jeremiah a difficult ministry (verse 10).

## b.	God's Promise to Defend and Protect Jeremiah

Jeremiah's call to become a prophet to nations came early in life and scared him terribly. He failed to match God's call with divine empowerment. Whenever God calls you to do something, He always provides the backing and empowerment to fulfill that calling.

God said to Jeremiah:

For behold, I have made you this day, a fortified city and an iron pillar, and bronze walls, against the whole land – against the king of Judah, against the princes; against the priests, and against the people of the land. They will fight against you but they shall not prevail against you; for I am with you, says the Lord; "to deliver you". Jeremiah 1:18, 19

## c.	Jeremiah's	Discouragement	and Complaint

Jeremiah encountered a lot of opposition and threat to his life (Jer. 11:18-29), his brothers and other family members dealt treacherously with him (Jer. 12:6); false prophets conspired against him (Jer. 28:10-11). Unfortunately, the people believed the false prophets and despised Jeremiah. God did not allow him to marry (Jer. 16:2). Solitude was at once his penalty for greatness. He encountered sad antagonisms (Jer. 20:1-18), therefore his ministry became unpopular. Jeremiah complained to the Lord:

O Lord, you induced me, and I was persuaded; You are stronger than I, and have prevailed, I am in derision daily; everyone mocks me. For I spoke, I cried out; I shouted, "violence and plunder!" Because the word of the Lord was made to me a reproach and a derision daily Jeremiah 20: 7, 8

Perhaps Jeremiah felt disappointed because, in spite of God's promise to protect him, he did not experience protection (Jer. 38: 1-6).

Jeremiah had faithfully proclaimed the Word as commissioned by God. But, instead of being encouraged, he was constantly persecuted by his people. He was a couple of times locked up in prison and he decided to "resign" from the ministry: "Then I said, I will not make mention of him, nor speak any more in his name" (Jer. 20:9a). Like Jeremiah, every leader experiences both good and bad days. Though Jeremiah complained in the first ten verses of

Jeremiah Chapter 20, he praised God in the next four verses for his victories.

d.   Jeremiah's Renewal

Jeremiah experienced a fresh touch from God, which renewed his passion for ministry.

But His word was in my heart like a burning fire shut up in my bones; I was weary of holding it back, and I could not. Jeremiah 20: 9b

The effect of this renewal:
-        Fresh zeal
-        Fresh fire
-        Fresh anointing
-        Fresh determination
-        Fresh courage

But the Lord is with me as a mighty, awesome one. Therefore my persecutors will stumble, and will not prevail. They will be greatly ashamed, for they will not prosper, their everlasting confusion will never be forgotten.   Jeremiah 20:11

e.   He sang a new song

His "old song" of complaining was replaced with a new song, a song of praise.

Sing to the Lord! Praise the Lord! For He has delivered the life of the poor from the hand of evil doers. Jeremiah 20:13

When our bad days come as leaders we should remember that God's greatest leaders became discouraged. We should rise above self-pity; failure is an attitude, not just an outcome. In time like this, we should think positively because success comes by going from failure to failure without losing enthusiasm. We make many mistakes; therefore we should learn from our mistakes because failure is not failures unless you learn nothing from it.

Quitting because of discouragement is not an option for good leaders because quitters never win, they are failures and let-down to their subordinates and admirers.

Therefore, when you fail, try, again, for God will rekindle a fresh zeal, fresh fire and fresh anointing in you to do new exploits. Cultivate a new attitude of "no quitting, no surrender" from today as God is ready to refire and recommission you.

The Egyptian Servant

a.   The Background

David and his men were living in Ziglag the land of Philistines as fugitives, as David fled from King Saul who was after his life. But war

165

broke out between Israel and the Philistines. David and his men came to assist the Philistines to fight against Israel but when the princes of the Philistines saw David they queried King Achish: "What are these Hebrews doing here especially David the servant of Saul?" The princes of the Philistines could not trust the loyalty of David as they suspected that he could turn against them in the battle field to appease his master, Saul. Consequently, King Achish advised David and his men to return to their camp; but on their return, they discovered that their wives and children had been taken away, while their personal effects were looted and their camp set ablaze by invading army of Amalekites (See I Sam. 29: 1-11; 30: 1-3).

David and his men were devastated, they wept profusely for the losses but David encouraged himself in the Lord who told him to pursue their looters, assuring him that he would overtake them and recover all (1 Sam. 30:6-8). Consequently, David and four hundred of his men pursued while two hundred men who were weary stayed behind. (1 Sam. 30:9-10).

b.   An Egyptian Found

David's men found an Egyptian along the way and brought him to David.

Then they found an Egyptian in the field, and brought him to David; and they gave

him bread and he ate, and they let him drink water. And they gave him a piece of a cake of figs and two clusters of resins. 1 Sam. 30:11

*   He was a servant of an Amalekite who raided Ziklag.
*   He was used and abandoned – left to die
*   He was sick and hungry – almost dead when David found him
*   He was at the right place at the right time

c.   The Egyptian Renewed

David revived him with bread and water. He had not had anything to eat or drink for three days. So they gave him some bread to eat and water to drink and his strength soon returned.

So when he had eaten, his strength came back to him; for he had eaten no bread nor drunk water for three days and three night   1 Sam. 30:12

He was renewed "and when he had eaten, his strength came again to him" (1 Sam 30:12b).

d.   The Renewed Egyptian

The ruthless Amamlekites left him to die, but God revived him and made him live. They used and dumped him, but God developed him. To the Amalekites, he was finished and useless, but God made him a useful vessel.

God can renew anyone and make that person useful and relevant. You may have been used, dumped and left to die; but God is able to renew, revive and restore you; He can use you again, and make you a blessing to your family, the church and your generation. You may have been ignored, no one appreciates your contribution, your date with destiny is near, you can be recognized and lifted from grass to glory, like Modecai.

e.   The Egyptian's New Mission

Before he was discovered by David, he was a servant used by the Amalekites. But after his renewal, he became faithful and useful to God and His people. Indeed, God did "a new thing" in his life.

The renewed Egyptian led David to the camp of the enemy after David and his men had treated him kindly. And he returned the kindness by being faithful to David; he led David to the place where the Amalekites were hiding.

And David said to him; can you take me down to the troop? So he said, swear to me by God that you will neither kill me nor deliver me into the hands of my master, and I will take you down to the troop. And when he had brought him down, there they were spread out over all the land, eating and drinking and dancing, because of all the great spoil which they had taken from the land of the Philistines and from the land of Judah 1 Samuel 30:15, 16

f. The Restoration: David Recovered All

Then David attacked them from twilight until the evening of the next day. Not a man of them escaped, except four hundred young men who rode on camels and fled. So David recovered all that the Amalekites had carried away, and David rescued his two wives. And nothing of theirs was lacking, either small or great, sons or daughters, spoil or anything which they had taken from them; David recovered all. Then David took all the flocks and herds they had driven before those other flock, and said, "this is David's spoil" 1 Samuel 30:17-20

David was one of the greatest leaders in the Old Testament; he trained 'losers' – men in distress, debtors, and discontented – to become an effective army. He was a builder of people, unlike Saul who was a user of people and never produced any leader. As a caring leader, David fed the used and abandoned Egyptian servant who eventually led the way to the flushing out of the rascals. He became the nemesis of the selfish and self-centred master and his team of looters.

This is a reminder to leaders to live exemplary lives, they should love and show kindness to their followers. Leaders should make the welfare of subordinates their priority. A used and dumped follower may tomorrow become the proverbial rejected stone that becomes the cornerstone of the house. Don't judge a person by what he is today because the future is in the hand of God. Who knows the table may turn the other way in favour of a today's servant.

Leaders should be guided by the golden rule:

"Therefore, whatever you want men to do to you, do also to them..." Matt. 7:12

BIBLIOGRAPHY

1.   Adams, Jay E., The Christian Case Book, Michigan: Baker Book House, 1979.

2.   Christopher, G. A., Arise And Shine, Lagos: World Missionary Gospel Church, 2014.

3.   Collins English Thesaurus, Glasgow: Herper Collins Publisher, 2011

4.   Commentary On The Whole Bible, Jamieson, R., Fausset, A. R., and Brown David, Michigan: Zondervan Publishing House, 1961.

5.   Dictionary of Pentecostal And Charismatic Movements, Michigan: Zondervan Publishing House, 1989.

6.   Henry, Mathew, Mathew Henry's Commentary On The Whole Bible, London: Marshall Pickering, 1960.

7.   Liardon, Robert, God's Generals, Tulsa, OK: Albury Pub.,1966.

8.   Maxwell C. John, The 21 Irrefutable Laws of Leadership, Nashville: Thomas Nelson Publisher, 1998.

9.   Maxwell C. John, The 5 Levels of Leadership, New York: Hachette Book Group, 2011.

10.   Maxwell C. John The 15 Invaluable Laws of Growth, New York: Hachette Book Group, 2012.

11.   Meduoye Felix, Making Maximum Impact, Lagos: Foursquare Gospel Church, 2014.

12.   Peale, Vincent Norman, The Power of Positive Thinking, New York: Simon & Schuster Inc,. 1980.

13.   Strong James, The Strong's Exhaustive Concordance of the Bible, Nashville: Thomas Nelson Publishers, 1978.

14.   The Concise English Dictionary, London: Oxford University Press, 1961.

15.   The New Encylopedia of Christian Quotations, Hamshire: John Hunt Publishing Ltd., 2000.

16.   Thomas, Choo, Heaven Is Real, Florida: Creation House Press, 1982.

17.   Vine, W. E., Vine's Expository Dictionary of New Testament Words, Massachusetts: Hendrickson Publishers, (no date).

18.   Zondervan's Pictorial Bible Dictionary, Michigan: Zondervan Publishing House, 1967.

ABOUT THE BOOK

This book "Season of New Beginnings" is a timely message from God to His church; it is of a profound, prophetic exposition of God's promise, through Prophet Isaiah, to "do a new thing" and its application to the Church in this End time. This book is about a new Season, the perfect season, the season of new beginnings, of restoration and hope, with new opportunities for a fresh start, fresh oil, fresh fire, fresh anointing, fresh passion and fresh power to surround new challenges and to do great exploits extraordinarily.

God may have done some great miracles in the past, but He will yet do greater things. He will "do a new thing" that will overshadow all your past exploits and breakthroughs. This is the 'season'; the season to favour you (Psalm 102:13), which will usher you into the realm of a new beginning with God; it will close doors to old things-old failure, old songs and open doors-better doors, doors to new things. This book will help you to "forget old things" and expect and receive "new things".

This powerful book will change you! It will change everything about you; it will profoundly, positively and permanently touch and renew your life, ministry, health, relationships or family.

You will be propelled with new strength beyond your natural limits, beyond your "old" strength; thus you can actualize your Divine destiny.

www.ingramcontent.com/pod-product-compliance
Lightning Source LLC
Chambersburg PA
CBHW071440090426
42737CB00011B/1724